Boxing for Self-Defense

Taking the Sweet Science from the Ring to the Street

Boxing for Self-Defense

Taking the Sweet Science from the Ring to the Street

Wim Demeere

Copyright 2019 by Wim Demeere

All rights reserved. No portion of this book may be reproduced, stored in a retrieval system, or transmitted in any form or by any means without express written permission of the publisher.

Published by Wim Demeere

Also by Wim Demeere

Books:

The Fighter's Guide to Hard-Core Heavy Bag Training

Timing in the Fighting Arts

The Fighter's Body

Martial Arts, Self-Defense and a Whole Lot More: The Best of Wim's Blog, Volume 1

The Leg Kick: Your Ultimate Guide to Using The Leg Kick for Mixed Martial Arts

Videos:

Combat Sanshou: The Punishing Chinese Fighting Art, Part One: Striking

Combat Sanshou: The Punishing Chinese Fighting Art, Part Two: Kicking

Combat Sanshou: The Punishing Chinese Fighting Art, Part Three: Takedowns, Throws, and Finishing Moves

Combat Sanshou: The Punishing Chinese Fighting Art, Part Four: Tiger & Snake

The Fighter's Video Guide to Hard-Core Heavy Bag Training

Pad Man, A Video Guide to Full-Contact Partner Training

Power/Control

Basic Self-Defense 1: Controlling Techniques

Stretching and Mobility Exercises for Martial Arts and Self-Defense

For an up to date page with direct links to all these books and videos, please go to this page on my website:

http://www.wimsblog.com/products

To Lauren and Xander. I couldn't be prouder of you both if I tried.

To Doug Patt. The Guardian at my abyss. It is my great fortune that I was a small part of your life and you a large one of mine. The world is darker without you. Rest in peace, my friend.

Contents

Introduction 1

Chapter One: Nuts and Bolts 5

Chapter Two: Getting started 31

Chapter Three: Basic offense 53

Chapter Four: Basic Defense 69

Chapter Five: Basic Clinching 85

Chapter Six: Goals and Tactics 101

Chapter Seven: Common mistakes 113

Conclusion 119

Author's note 121

About the Author 123

Acknowledgments

I couldn't have written this book without some others, so their help deserves to be recognized:

My lovely lady. Thank you for your patience and understanding. Your support means the world to me.

My student, Karsten Turf. Thank you for your patience while making the pictures for this book.

My Patrons at https://www.patreon.com/wimdemeere for all their support and feedback. In particular, to Andy Benfield, Gerry Schiela, Eric Shaver and Eric Parsons.

Introduction

I love boxing. I've been a fan of the noble art of self-defense for as long as I can remember. Some of my fondest childhood memories are of watching great fighters like Marvin Hagler, Roberto Duran and Sugar Ray Leonard wage war on the television screen. These bouts aired late at night and I would replay them in my mind after I was sent to bed by my father. The champions of the ring seemed larger than life, more comic book superheroes than simple mortals. The way they strived to outsmart, outfight and outlast each other left a lasting impression on me. Most of all, it made me want to train in combat sports.

For numerous reasons, I ended up taking the path of martial arts and self-defense instead of boxing and I have trained hard in several such disciplines for over thirty years now. But I never stopped seeing boxing as one of the most formidable fighting arts in the world.

To put that in perspective: despite all my experience in Eastern martial arts, when my son wanted to start training, I taught him boxing *first*.

I believe that just like you don't know kicking until you've been kicked by a Muay Thai fighter, you don't know striking until you've been punched by a boxer. Western boxing is not inferior to any Eastern martial art when it comes to striking and, in several cases, I consider it superior. However, it is also limited by its modern rules and limitations which makes it less suited for today's self-defense needs.

For example, in previous centuries, many a gentleman learned boxing not as an isolated sport, but in conjunction with other arts: wrestling, fencing, staff fighting, etc. The standard was that you trained to defend yourself in all ranges of combat, both armed and unarmed. Eventually, modern boxing and its restrictive rules replaced this practice and those aspects of fighting were put aside. Today, hardly any boxer understands the connections between pugilism and those other arts.

I don't intend to resurrect the old pugilism techniques in this book, even though it might seem that way sometimes. On the contrary, my goal is to reach two specific types of reader:

- Those of you who want to use boxing for self-defense, because that is what you have available to you, or it is what you want to do. This means you're a beginner with no other training.
- Those of you who already have training in modern ring boxing. It doesn't matter if you compete or not, you already have experience with boxing techniques and want to use them for self-defense too.

If you're in this second category, here is a word of caution.

Training in "dirty" boxing and developing the mindset to use your techniques for self-defense is radically different from fighting in the ring: the techniques are different and so is the environment. But the need to ingrain your techniques, tactics and mindset remains the same and this will influence your sports boxing techniques. As you know from your current training, if you don't ingrain techniques in practice, they won't magically appear in the ring. The same is true for dirty boxing techniques; if you ingrain them, they will interfere with your sports boxing techniques and mindset. I believe, to a certain degree, sports boxing and dirty boxing are incompatible.

It is perfectly acceptable to instinctively grab your attacker's face and twist his neck to break his grip when you must defend yourself in the street; in the ring, this gets you disqualified. Do that enough times and you get a reputation for being a dirty fighter. This makes it hard to develop a career as an amateur or as a professional fighter.

I advise you to carefully think things through before training in the illegal boxing techniques in this book.

As an aside, even if you don't compete, your sparring partners will not appreciate you using prohibited techniques. Depending on how things go, they might be content with "teaching you a lesson" or you might get kicked out of the gym. Either way, that's not something you want.

To be clear, it is not impossible to control the types of techniques you use in sparring or in a prize fight and some people manage this just fine. There are fighters who have enough experience to not revert to illegal blows when they are put under pressure. If you're not at that level, you risk reacting with dirty boxing when things get intense. Remember that you ingrain the street boxing techniques for exactly this type of situation: when you're under attack and have to react instinctively…

That's why I cover primarily *the standard boxing techniques* in this book; the jab, cross, hook, etc. I focus on how to adapt these to defend yourself outside of the ring. By working with techniques you already know (or learn first if you're a beginner), we can hopefully avoid that conflict between ring and street boxing. This is not only safer, but it also means you need less training time to adapt your techniques to the new context.

In the second volume of this book series, I'll exclusively write about all the dirty tricks and techniques that would get you barred for life by any professional boxing association should you use them in the ring. That book will be written with the assumption that you have done the training in the following chapters, or you no longer have any interest in sports boxing. Then we can take the gloves off and get downright nasty!

For now, I want to help you transition from *the ring to the street*. I'll show you where things are different, what to watch out for and what remains the same. If you train hard, then you can learn to transfer your skills to the arena that is the street.

You might have doubts about this division between fighting in the ring and outside of it, so let's look a bit deeper:

Is there a difference between boxing as a combat sport and boxing for self-defense?

Yes, and there are many factors involved. I won't go into all of them, but ask yourself this question: *How often does a boxing match end with a KO in three to ten seconds? Or in thirty seconds?*

Sure, it happens, but it's much more common that the fight goes on for several rounds or goes the distance.

Here's another question: *How many self-defense situations last the same amount of time as a boxing match?*

This is *extremely* rare.

I'll post some video examples in the resources page to illustrate this, but in a true self-defense context, the violence is typically sudden, extreme and over quickly:

- In a road rage incident, a furious motorist gets out of his car and starts kicking yours. You get out to stop him but before you can fully exit your vehicle, he rushes in and pins you with the car door. You're stuck and unable to defend yourself well while he rains down punches on you.
- A guy gets angry with you in a bar and suddenly launches a full-power sucker punch. If you don't block it or move your head, you'll be out on your feet and the next few punches will finish the job.

- A tweaker gets in your face to hide the fact that his buddy is coming up behind you. That guy hits you in the back of the head with a brick, you go down and they stomp you just long enough so you can't stop them from taking your wallet.

These are just a handful of examples to illustrate that the environment in which you use boxing techniques for self-defense is radically different from ring fighting. By definition (and I'll get back to this in the next chapter), self-defense cannot be mutual combat. The concept of a *prolonged engagement with an opponent* doesn't apply.

Another reason why you don't want things to take a few rounds is that the longer the fight takes, the higher the odds of:

- Your attacker landing a shot and you going down. There is no referee to stop him once you're on the ground
- One of his friends gets involved and blindsides you
- He either pulls a weapon or uses an improvised weapon found nearby

There's more, but this should suffice to convince you that to use your boxing for self-defense, you need to switch mindsets from *competition* to *survival*. The tactics and mindset of constructing a victory gradually and slowly whittling away your opponent or winning on points is perfect for the ring.

It doesn't apply to self-defense.

A different way of fighting is necessary and in the following chapters and the two upcoming volumes of this book series, we go into detail on everything that entails.

Important:

Throughout the book, I reference the "Resources Page". This is a page on my website created specifically for this book. I put everything on there that won't fit in this book: videos, links to other sites, equipment and more. Please go to wimdemeere.com/boxing to view the page and all the content there.

Chapter One: Nuts and Bolts

Before you can successfully use your techniques in the street, there are several vitally important concepts you need to understand and ingrain. Doing so not only makes you more effective, it also helps you stay out of jail should you need to use your training. We have to cover a lot of ground, but let's start with the most important part:

When can you throw a punch in self-defense?

What is self-defense?

Before you read on, here's a caveat: It is your responsibility to research the self-defense and use of force laws that govern your area. Also, as I'm not a lawyer, I can't give you legal advice.

What I can do is point out the elements that consistently come up in the legal systems of most modern countries. Though the details vary, you could do worse than keep these in mind and adjust your training accordingly. Explaining the full ramifications of these legal issues is beyond the scope of this book, but you'll at least have an idea of where to start your research. Should you neglect to do so, get into a fight you think was self-defense and are proven wrong, don't get upset if you end up in jail. You were warned…

Here are some of the key factors you need to understand:

- **Unprovoked attack.** If you start the altercation, you usually aren't acting in self-defense in the eyes of the law. Though there are some exceptions, it is safer to assume they don't apply to your situation.

- **Imminent threat.** You're in danger *right now*. Not in a few minutes or in a few days, *now*. A guy threatening to beat you up next time he sees you doesn't justify violence as far as the law is concerned.

- **Reasonable fear.** The threat needs to be real and not just exist in your imagination. If you're a 30-year old 250-pound professional boxer, it's not reasonable to be afraid of a 10-year old kid weighing in at a whopping 80 pounds. The disparity of force is just too big for this to be the case.

- **Duty to retreat/avoidance.** In some jurisdictions, you're obligated to try and avoid the confrontation before it turns violent, if possible. Failing to do so can negate your claim of self-defense.

- **Castle doctrine.** This is an exception to the previous rule: if you're attacked in your home, there is no longer a duty to retreat.

- **Proportionality and reasonable use of force.** If somebody slaps you in the face, you can't punch him in the throat until his larynx is turned into pulp and he suffocates. The violence you use in response to an attack has to be reasonable and in proportion to the level of violence used against you.

- **Pre-emptive striking.** This one is tricky. In theory, it is allowed in many legal systems. In practice, it gets complicated and can be used against you. Research what applies to your neck of the woods.

- **Reasonable man standard.** This legal concept is used as a standard to which citizens are held. The law looks at the incident and asks the question: *what would a reasonable person have done in your place?* If your actions don't rhyme with those of that hypothetical reasonable person, you just might be in trouble.

This is not a complete list, nor is it meant to be. It is a basic introduction to the complexities you encounter when you claim self-defense. To that end, understand this:

Just reading and understanding this list doesn't make you an expert on this topic. I've been studying and researching it for more than thirty years and still don't consider myself an expert, because it is such a vast and complex subject. Every single one of the bullets in the above list needs qualifiers, nuances and there are many exceptions an average civilian cannot interpret correctly. That is why I not only urge you to talk to a lawyer who pleads self-defense cases (not one who does divorce cases or any other aspect of practicing law; you need a specialist), but also a police officer. Things get complicated real fast. Here's why:

- **Depending on circumstances, the police might get involved.** Once they do and decide to take you back to the station, you enter the legal system. At best, you're forced to spend several hours in a police station being processed: finger-printed, recorded, placed in a cell, etc. If you're lucky, you're released soon after. If not, you might not be able to get back to your life for a long time. You could lose your job, your relationships and all your savings while the system keeps you away from civilian life.

- **People lie.** They don't always do so with malicious intent, but lie they do. That guy who got in your face and tried to sucker punch you, but you knocked him out instead? When he wakes up, he's going to claim *you* started it all. The police officers who show up at the scene cannot know who is right, so they often take both parties into custody and sort things out back at the police station. That means interrogations and lots of questions you have to answer correctly before they believe you acted in self-defense. Lots of opportunities to mess this up…

- **Witnesses lie too.** Witnesses are unreliable and lie as well, on purpose or otherwise. For instance, some people only saw the part where you punched the guy and not him trying to sucker punch you. They'll claim *you* were the aggressor. It is not a lie to them; they'll swear to it on a bible in a court of law, because it is what they saw. It isn't the full truth though, not the way you experienced it.

- **Expect to be recorded.** We live in a time where cameras are everywhere. CCTV systems are all over the place and people record fights on their cell phones all the time. The footage can be used against you if it isn't consistent with your claim of self-defense. As you can expect by now, the camera lies too. Depending on the quality of the video, the camera angle, when the footage starts, etc., a video can make you look guilty when you're not.

- **It costs money.** If the guy you knocked out takes a bad fall and fractures his skull when he hits the pavement, all bets are off. If he doesn't die, you're probably looking at having to pay for his medical expenses. If he does die, you can expect to go to trial for homicide. That means hiring a criminal defense lawyer and they cost tens of thousands of dollars.

- **It can get political.** Suppose you get arrested, the police believe your claim of self-defense, and they want to let you walk. Unfortunately, they can't because it's an election year for the district attorney and he doesn't want to look weak on crime. So, he decides to make an example out of you and prosecutes you to the full extent of the law.

Once again, this list isn't complete. These are but a few of the complications that can get you in trouble with the legal system, even if you haven't done anything wrong. Life isn't fair and anything can happen, so it is in your best interest to understand what you legally can and cannot do using the boxing techniques in this book.

If after all the above you still don't care about this, please re-read the title of this book. It doesn't say "Boxing for Bullies" or "Boxing for Violent Assholes." It says "Boxing for Self-Defense".

Please go to the resources page for a list of books I recommend for more information on this topic and some videos examples of what is *not* self-defense.

Which is best: Open hand or closed fist striking?

One of those recurring arguments in self-defense circles revolves around open hand versus closed fist striking. I've heard too many people parrot theories without thinking them through. It won't surprise you that I believe things are more nuanced than these black/white statements. Here's the best known one:

Hard weapon to soft target, soft weapon to hard target.

The idea is: if you use a fist, punch a soft target like the stomach instead of the face to avoid breaking your knuckles on the hard bones of the skull. If you want to hit a hard surface, they insist you use a softer weapon, like an open hand strike.

This is by no means bad advice, but it isn't written in stone. For the average person and, in particular, a person not interested in spending lots of time training, this works just fine. Hell, it works just fine if you've been training for decades, so you won't hear me argue against this rule. Also, having suffered the infamous "Boxer's fracture" when I was thirteen (apparently, solid wood doesn't break easily…) I understand fully well how a poorly placed punch can send you to the hospital.

What I argue against is the implied assumptions that come with it and the dogma that surrounds it. There are several assumptions that people subconsciously adhere to when they claim this rule as absolute:

As if every single closed fist punch to a hard target results in a broken hand.

As if it's impossible to punch a hard target with a closed fist without injury to your fist.

As if every open hand strike ever thrown has a 100% no-injury track record.

As if you cannot injure your open hand striking a hard target.

This is not necessarily stated openly, but it is all too often implied in their reasoning and they train accordingly. Here's the thing: I know from personal experience that such absolute statements are complete nonsense. I want to explore some of the factors that are typically overlooked but are nonetheless of critical importance.

1) Five types of impact

I learned about the five types of impact in an old Bushido manual some 25 years ago. It changed the way I trained forever. I wrote about this in detail in my *Hardcore Heavy Bag Training* book and demonstrate the concepts in detail in my *Combat Sanshou: Striking* video. For an in-depth explanation, I suggest you get those as I only cover them briefly here. The links are on the resources page.

Let's go over them:

- **Penetrating:** The kind you use to break boards or kick in a door. It travels *through* the target as if to break it. This is what most practitioners think of when they speak about striking power.
- **Shockwave:** The weapon lands and sticks. It is fired much like a penetrating impact, but it doesn't aim to go as deep. When it lands, it delivers the kinetic energy to a relatively large area.
- **Bouncing:** The weapon hits and uses the impact to recoil quickly along the path it came. Think of it as throwing a ball at a wall to make it bounce back to you. Another example is how many beginning boxers use their jab.
- **Ricochet:** Similar to bouncing impact but instead of reversing the direction 180°, the weapon shoots off at a different angle after it lands. For instance, 90°.
- **Ripping:** Picture slashing through a target with a sword. The weapon lands at an oblique angle, strikes the target and is then dragged across to come out the other end. A good example is ripping hook punches to the body.

There is overlap between these categories depending on how you strike, the kind of technique used, etc. But they offer a practical framework to determine *how* and *why* you use certain techniques: the type of impact determines *the potential for damage to your hand* when you use an open hand or closed fist. It also determines the kinds of results you get when the strike lands. Two examples:

- You can probably hit somebody in the face with a bouncing backfist all day long without breaking your knuckles. In contrast, a dozen or so maximum power straight punches with penetrating impact to somebody's skull most likely leave your fist all broken and mangled.
- A penetrating palm heel strike to an attacker's face is likely to rock his head back and leave your hand just fine. That same penetrating palm heel at a slightly downward angle targeted at the sternum can break your wrist. How do I know? Because I busted my scaphoid when I did just that some twenty years ago and the surgeon explained the mechanics of the break to me. It took 5 months in a cast and surgery to fix.

There are many more examples, but you get the point: there is more than one way of striking and each one yields different results. If somebody claims, "You always have to hit through the target!" or insists you "Aim every punch at the back of his head!" then he doesn't understand this is only valid for penetrating impact. It is not good advice for the four other types of impact, yet it's often taught as a universal truth. But it's simply wrong.

Practicing, understanding and ingraining the five types of impact is the key to consistent effective striking.

2) Target

The target your punch lands on also plays a major role in determining to strike with an open hand or a closed fist. Yet, it is often seen as one homogenous whole, instead of the more complex topic it actually is. Some knowledge of basic anatomy can be a good thing.

First, there's the human head, which is comprised of multiple components. Each one has a different function and density, resulting in different best practices regarding the use of different hand configurations and types of impact. For example:

- Hitting the frontal bone is not the same as hitting the temporal bone. The former is much denser and striking it hard in a linear fashion tends to lead to broken knuckles. The temporal bone is more vulnerable due to its shape, location and density. I still wouldn't hit it with penetrating power with a closed fist, but shockwave works just fine for me.

- Hitting the mandible close to the neck from the side is not the same as striking the tip of the chin from that angle. In the former, the impact tends to move the head to the side more than anything else. If you're unlucky, you just broke your fist. But if you throw the same technique at the tip of the chin, odds are good you'll rotate his head which allows your fist to travel through unharmed.

Next, if you hit an unsupported target, the impact is different than when it is supported. For example, punching somebody in the head when he's standing in front of you yields different results than when you pin his head against a wall and use that same punch. In the first case, some of the energy bleeds off due to his head moving on impact. In the second, his head absorbs all the force, and because of Newton's third law, your fist is under a lot more pressure on impact and might get damaged.

3) Angle of attack

The vector or angle of attack your fist or open hand follows matters a great deal. I'll gladly use a closed fist at a slightly downward angle on the side of the tip of the chin, because that angle makes it likely my opponent's head tilts away from my fist and doesn't damage it. I'll absolutely avoid that same angle with a fist if the target is the frontal bone. But I'd again gladly use that angle on the frontal bone with a shock wave impact using an open hand.

There are too many angles of attack to discuss in detail here, but that doesn't mean there aren't other possibilities than what I just wrote above. The key to keeping your fist safe is to align the angle of attack and your knuckles with the surface of impact. An easy exercise to understand this is this:

Stand in front of a wall and extend your arm as if throwing a jab. Place your knuckles against the wall the way you want them to be when you land that jab on an attacker.

Now lift your arm an inch or two without bending your elbow. Notice how you now can't touch the wall correctly, but instead you make contact with the wrong knuckles. These break if you punch with even just a bit of power.

This is an example of how a technique (jab) needs to hit a specific surface (flat and vertical) along the right angle of attack so you don't break your hand. Now apply the same principle to all your punches and all targets. Experiment slowly hitting specific targets with specific techniques, so you learn to deliver powerful blows without injuring yourself.

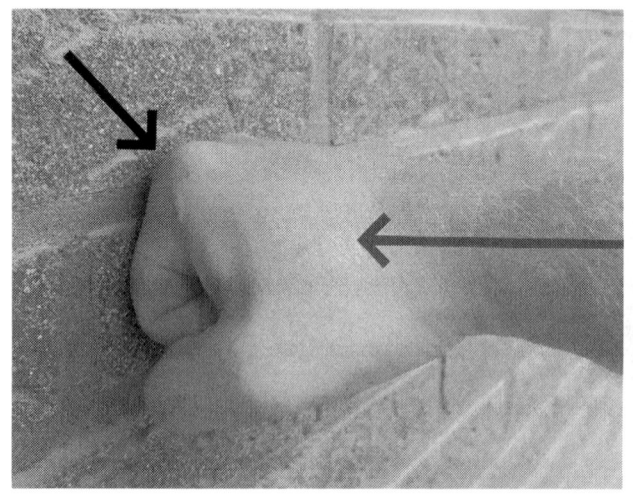

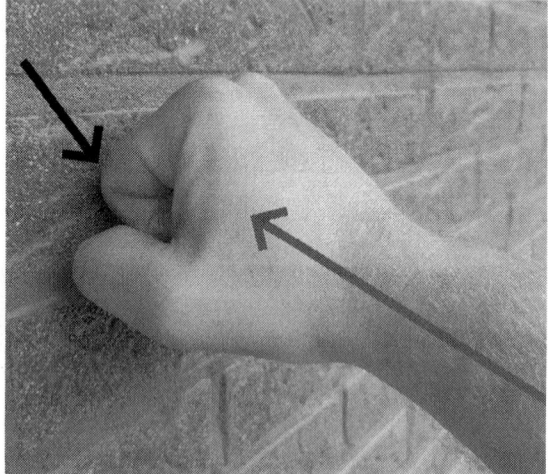

4) Body type

We're all built differently: the shape of your skeleton, where your muscles insert on each joint (and the leverage (dis)advantage it gives), the ratio of different types of muscle fibres, the length of each bone, the density of your bones, etc. All of these vary wildly from one person to the next. The only way to know those details is extensive medical testing, which most people never do until they get sick or injured.

For instance, I have a bad back. I never knew it until they took an MRI of my spine because of the chronic pain. Turns out the shape of my vertebrae isn't that great and the canal my spinal cord has to travel through is narrower than average. This hasn't stopped me from training extremely hard for the past thirty years, but it does have implications as I get older.

The same goes for one of the critical factors in choosing an open hand or a closed fist to strike: bone density. Some people naturally have thick and strong bones whereas others are cursed with fragile ones. This is partly why some people can punch a guy in the face with a closed fist and never break their hand, whereas others break it every time they try. That said, bone density changes as you age (they get more brittle) so don't go thinking you're off the hook if your bones are solid as rock right now.

5) Luck

You can throw the same technique twice in similar circumstances and get completely different results:

- I threw a left hook at a student's head during sparring and he wasn't quick enough to duck, so my punch landed flush on his forehead. It was a relatively hard punch and I was wearing 12 oz boxing gloves, but I still broke my knuckle. My student, on the other hand, was fine, it didn't even phase him.
- In another session, I threw the same left hook at a sparring partner. I didn't feel any impact and thought I missed, but he dropped unconscious to the floor in front of me. I had apparently just barely clipped him on the chin, but it was enough to turn off his lights. I was wearing the same gloves.

Same punch, same circumstances. Completely different results. There are no guarantees in a fight, it is all up in the air at any given time.

In conclusion, I'd like to add the following:

There's more to the debate than this. I could have gone on about specific hand configurations and body mechanics, but this is already long enough. The point is that a standard "Hard weapon to soft target, soft weapon to hard target" reply is at best, incomplete and at worst, misleading or a flat out lie. It is a good starting point for your training, and you could do a lot worse than sticking to it. But don't fall into the trap of thinking it is an absolute rule. Many other factors can change the dynamics and therefore the results of landing a technique. Bear in mind that just because something doesn't work for you, doesn't mean it can't work for somebody else.

Generating power

In this section, I only focus on a basic way of generating power. There is a lot more to it, but the more advanced information is beyond the scope of this book. Instead, I share a basic method that works under the extreme stress of an actual fight, providing you ingrain it correctly. Let's look at the two primary components:

1) Rotation

Consider this sequence of techniques: jab-cross-lead hook-rear hook. This is a standard combination in which you perform four of the most basic techniques in boxing. I'd like you to try it from a regular fighting stance in front of the mirror. Or make a video of yourself on your cell phone and watch the footage afterwards.

Focus on the movement of your shoulders:

- Notice that your lead shoulder turns forward a little during the jab, whereas your rear shoulder retracts a bit. This lengthens your punch and increases the power by aligning all the joints behind your fist.
- With the cross, your entire body rotates in the opposite direction: your left shoulder turns back as your right shoulder turns forward.
- As you perform the lead hook, you reverse direction again: your left shoulder turns forward as your right shoulder turns back.
- Finally, with the rear hook, your left shoulder turns back again as your right shoulder turns forward.

This is the most basic form of generating power in boxing: quickly rotating your spine to the left and to the right. It seems too simple to be true, but you can generate tremendous power by concentrating on this rotational movement first. Then, connect your arm to that rotation and let your fist follow the desired path to the target. Voila, a powerful punch!

Here's an exercise you can do to improve your body mechanics with rotation:

- Let's assume that you're in a regular left lead stance. Make it slightly larger than usual, keeping your spine completely vertical and your knees bent a little bit more than normal. This puts you in a slightly deeper and longer stance.
- Next, place your feet at a 90° angle towards each other: your lead foot points straight forward and your back foot points 90° away from it. This feels awkward at first but don't worry about it.
- Fully rotate your upper body so your shoulders are aligned, pointing straight forward and backwards. Optionally, put your hands behind your back and clasp them together so you can't use them to aid the movement. This is the *open position*.
- Now rotate towards your left with your entire body until your right shoulder faces fully forward and your left shoulder fully back. Your shoulders should have completed a 180° turn. To allow this kind of rotation, you have to pick up your back heel while keeping the ball of your foot on the floor. Then bend your right knee, which in turn allows your right hip to turn forward. This lets your spine twist fully to your left so you can bring your right shoulder all the way up front. This is the **closed position** and it feels uncomfortable and difficult to hold at first. Do it anyway and stay therefore 3 to 4 seconds. The way you move your body just now is **closing rotation**.
- Rotate backwards, letting your right shoulder travel all the way back and bringing your left shoulder forward again, as your entire body torques in the opposite direction and you resume the open stance. This type of movement is **opening rotation**.

Practice this drill until you can do it fluidly and at speed while maintaining perfect balance and control. Then practice it again but sink a little bit lower into your stance than before. This gives your legs a good workout while it increases your balance, coordination, and maximum power. Train until you can once again do this at top speed without losing balance.

Only now do you add other movements to it: start by alternating left and right straight punches as you rotate into the open and closed position. When you can do that well, try the same thing with hooks and then uppercuts.

When you can do those correctly too, mix and match all the basic punching techniques while you rotate faster and faster.

Though in this drill you perform everything in largesse, you don't have to rotate 100% each time you throw a punch for real. The goal of the drill is to develop your physical skills as quickly as possible and for that, you start with maximum range of motion in each rotation. Later, you practice smaller rotations while working hard to maintain as much power as possible.

2) Momentum

Try this exercise: stand completely still in your fighting stance in front of your heavy bag, close enough to land the jab. Then snap out your fastest and hardest jab, hitting the heavy back square in the middle. How far back does the bag move?

Do the exercise again, but first take a step back from the heavy bag. Resume your fighting stance, focus and then step in, as you punch with the same speed and snap as before. What happens now? If you did it right, the bag moved back a lot more than the first time. This happens because the second time, you have momentum; your entire body is in motion as opposed to just your arm.

Now try the same drill with all your other basic techniques: first from a stationary position and then, strike as you advance. Notice the difference?

The physics of momentum are complex when you drill down into the details, so we won't go there. Suffice it to say that if you can move your entire body into it as you throw a punch, it adds tremendously to the power. That doesn't mean you can't hit hard without momentum, only that given the option, adding momentum usually makes it easier to hit with devastating power.

To do so you need balance and footwork. Balance allows you to move at high speed without overcommitting and falling over after you punch. Footwork lets you move explosively and generates lots of momentum that you can then add to your technique.

As you can probably guess, combining rotation and momentum is the recipe for knock out power in all your punches. My advice is to train them separately at first and then mix them together in varying degrees to develop sound body mechanics that generate bone-jarring impacts without much effort.

Range

Each weapon has a specific distance at which it can be used most effectively. For instance, the jab and the cross only work correctly when your opponent is relatively far away. The lead and rear uppercut work best when your opponent is a lot closer. The same applies to all techniques and their variations. Understanding range is a critical component of good striking; there is no way around it.

There are two main ways to define range:

1) Calculating the distance between you and your opponent to use a technique that is most efficient at this distance.

Here, range is described is as follows:

- You start outside of range; your opponent cannot even touch you with his furthest reaching technique. Imagine he doesn't move, no matter what you do.
- With one step towards him, you enter the distance that allows you to land techniques while still staying as far away as you can. This is long range, where straight punches like the jab and cross work best.
- Take another step forward and you get to medium range, which is where you throw the hook techniques.
- With one more step, we get to close range, where you throw short tight hooks and uppercuts.
- Sometimes the clinch is also seen as a separate range, one that comes after close range. Fighting from the clinch means you or your opponent are holding on to each other with at least one arm, or you have your head buried in his chest and are striking at extreme close range while he holds onto you.
- Notice how the lead foot is always a step closer when you cross over into the next range.

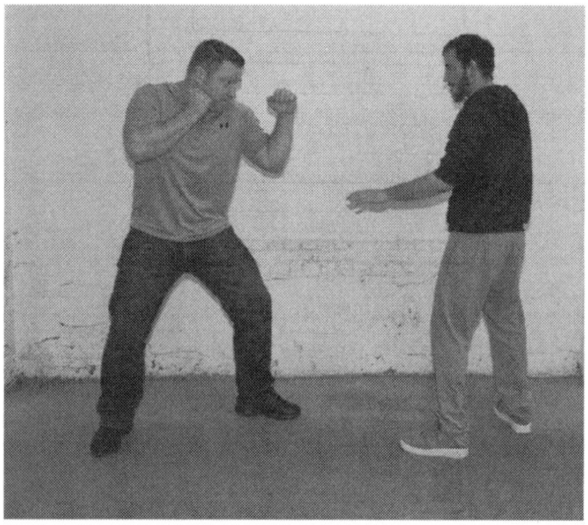

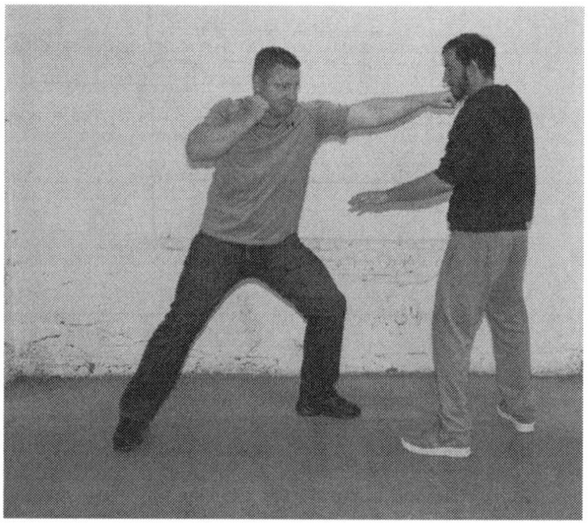

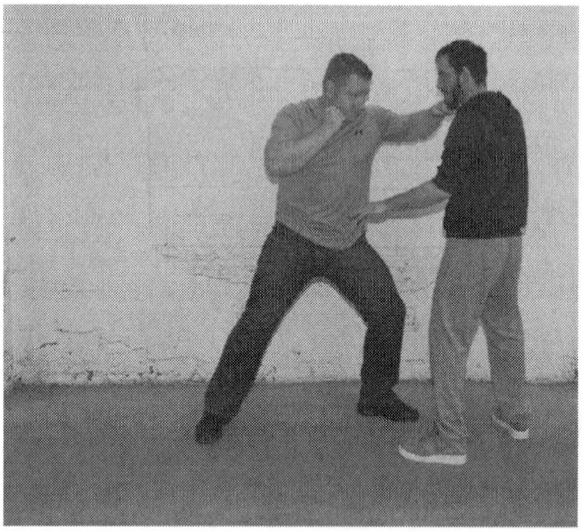

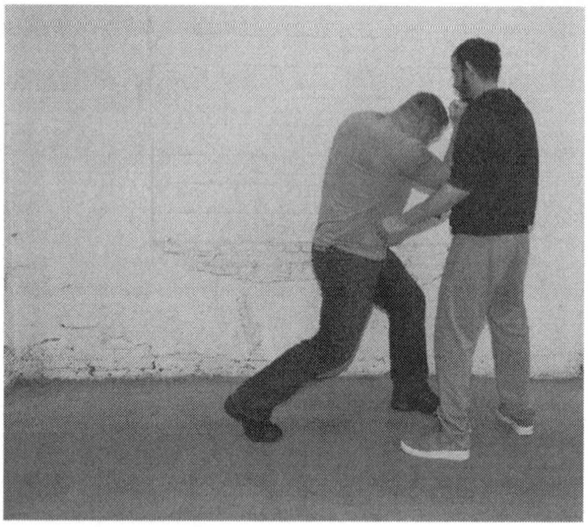

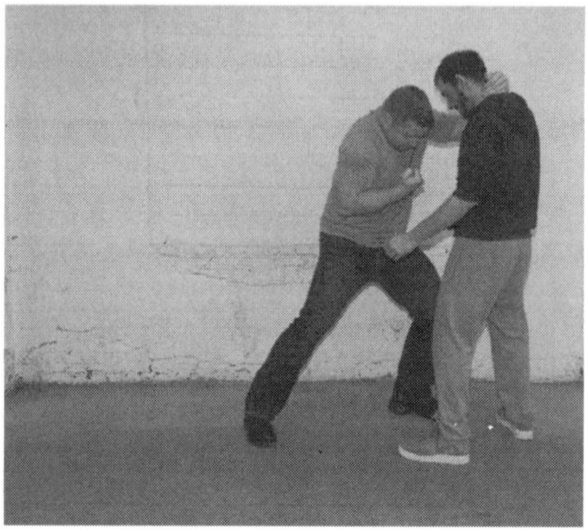

2) Range is the distance at which you can hit a specific target with a given technique.

In the first definition, you used footwork to cross each separate range as you closed in on your opponent: each step forward brought you closer and changed the techniques best used there. Contrast this with the following concept:

Whenever your opponent offers you a target, regardless of how far your feet are placed in relation to his, hit it with the appropriate technique.

Here's an example to make this clearer:

Picture you and your opponent at long range as described before. This time he doesn't just stand, but he leans forward as he uses head movement to be more elusive. As he's a bit too predictable with it, you spot his head coming forward at a slight angle. If you have good timing, you can then land a hook right before he retracts his head.

He moved his head closer to *you*. He changed the range so it was too close for a straight punch, but close enough for your hook to land. The key point is that he did not move his feet.

Viewed through the lens of the first definition, he was still at long range when he moved his head forward and therefor a jab or cross should have been appropriate. According to the second definition, his head moved into your medium range, so you threw a hook. In other words, his head came into medium range while his feet were still at long range.

This applies to you as well.

Let's assume the same scenario again: you're both at long range when you only look at the position of your feet. This time, you make the initial move: you feint with your right shoulder, as if throwing a cross and lean forward and slightly to your left. This brings you closer to your opponent than you normally would be for a straight punch. It also loads up the left hook. Now rotate your body again in an opening rotation and throw a lead hook to the body.

The only reason you managed to land this shot is because you leaned forward with your upper body, thereby closing the distance between you two.

These two ways of viewing range are complementary, and you should use them together instead of separately. Always interpret the ever-changing distance between you and your opponent so you can land with the best possible technique at any given moment. This improves your target selection and your technique selection. Eventually, you pick the perfect technique for whatever available targets you spot at any given moment.

There is still another important concept we need to address: *optimal range.* This means that every technique has range at which it works best. Don't make the mistake of thinking of this in absolute terms; it is a scale that starts on one side where the technique doesn't work at all, to the opposite side where it works perfectly. For example, look at the right cross:

Face your opponent in your fighting stance at the ideal distance for an advancing right cross. Take a step forward and throw it at his chin. Let's assume he didn't move and you manage to land it. You have good power generation, everything is aligned correctly, and the result is a powerful blow that knocks him out.

Now take this same scenario, but this time he leans in just as you as you throw the right cross. This shortens the distance between the starting point of your punch and where his head is now at. As a result, you only get to half-extend your arm in that right cross.

In the first case, you have optimal range, which is where everything works out: you have the ideal conditions to throw the punch, so it reaches its full potential when it lands.

In the second example, you landed the punch before you got to that point. However, just because you're not at the ideal range, that doesn't automatically mean it can't be an effective punch. If you generate enough power and speed, the result can still be more than enough to hurt or stop him. Obviously, you want to get as close as possible to optimal range with every single punch. If that isn't possible, you don't necessarily stop attacking and back off to start over. In self-defense there is no such thing as waiting for the right opportunity, again and again:

If you only fight defensively, you will lose.

This is a fundamental shift in mindset when going from sports-boxing to self-defense. There is only a short amount of time before things can and will go wrong in the street. You want to finish it ASAP instead of playing a long game over several rounds and score points.

If optimal range isn't accessible for whatever reason, settle for a less than perfect punch and don't stop attacking. If you ingrained good body mechanics, even a less than optimal strike hurts your opponent and gets results. Remember the old military maxim:

A good enough plan executed forcefully right now is better than the perfect plan executed a day late.

I can't stress enough the importance of a sense of urgency in a self-defense context. You don't have time and you need to end the altercation as fast as possible. Preferably, you're done with it in a few seconds.

This brings us to another point:

Though power and speed are critical in developing reliable self-defense techniques, other factors are equally important. Beginning fighters often focus on speed and power, as they are relatively easy to improve upon and therefor quickly yield impressive results:

- You can instantly hit harder if you throw your body into a punch, even if you end up off-balance.
- With just a few months of regular training, you can also improve your speed to a large degree.

It is easy to fool yourself into thinking you're badass once you start packing a decent punch. But what if you can't land it where it hurts the most? You also need the ability to land those shots where they do the most damage and that means *accuracy*.

If you train to have sniper-like precision with all your punches, then even less than optimal techniques can still be enough to stop your attacker. Remember that there are no weight classes in the street, so if you have to defend yourself against an attacker who outweighs you significantly, accurately hitting vulnerable targets may be the only thing that can get the job done.

Let's take a closer look at targeting and everything that comes with it.

Targeting

In the sport of boxing, the typical targets are the head and the body. What's more, you're only allowed to strike these from the front and the side. Several other interesting targets are off-limits:

- The back of the head.
- The back of the torso.
- All targets below the belt.
- The throat.

In self-defense there are no such limitations, so you have to adapt your targeting as well. Just to be clear, in this book, I don't focus on all those illegal targets. I will cover all the fouls and dirty boxing techniques in the second volume of this series on boxing for self-defense. Remember that this volume is focused on applying the boxing skills you've already acquired in a sports context for your self-defense use. Or, if you want to learn boxing from scratch but also use it for self-defense. In both cases, you're stuck with the limitations of boxing as a sport. The goal of this book is to teach you how to use those skills for self-defense.

Allow me to explain this a bit more before I go back to targeting.

One of the reasons why I split the subject into separate book volumes (aside of there being too much content for just one book), is to make the learning process easier and faster. If as a beginner, you already focus on hitting illegal targets, it can be confusing. You risk going for illegal targets when you train sports boxing and get kicked out of your gym. That is why I believe a sequential approach is more effective in the long run:

- First, develop sound fundamentals if you're new to boxing. Those that cross over from the ring to the street.
- If you already have those fundamentals, adjust them to the differences between the ring and the street as I explain them throughout this book.
- Only when you can do this consistently and under stress, then you can dig into all the dirty boxing and attack illegal targets.

With this approach, you first develop as strong core of fundamental boxing skills that you can use both inside and outside of the ring. The dirty boxing and attacking illegal targets are skills you then layer on top of that foundation. These give you more versatility and tools to use, but they also demand specific training. The downside is that this kind of training has a negative influence on how you box in the ring or in competition. As the old boxing adage goes: you fight the way you train.

Fighting should be as simple as you can possibly make it. I firmly believe in developing a strong foundation first and only adding more techniques on top of those when you have both the experience and the skill to do so. That is why the second volume will consider those additional techniques and targets, working from the assumption you already mastered everything written in this book.

If you want to get notified when those next books are released, join my mailing list at www.wimdemeere.com/notification. No spam, just an email when I have a new product out or do a discount.

All that said, let's dig into targeting.

You want to target parts of the human anatomy that consistently yield good results, which means making specific choices. These choices depend on context and the specific skills and tools you bring to the confrontation. There are different ways to look at this:

- First consider who you are and who your opponent is. If you're significantly smaller than him, certain targets are of no use to you. For instance, if he outweighs you by 100 pounds, jabbing him in the stomach is unlikely to get you far.
- Environmental factors. If you're attacked outside during winter, odds are good he's wearing a thick jacket. That means attacking the body is virtually useless, leaving head shots as the only option.
- How tall is he? There's a huge difference between having to strike upwards towards a taller opponent's head and hitting on a more horizontal line if you're both the same height. The same goes for hitting smaller opponents in a downward trajectory. Differences in height require specific training to maintain your accuracy, or you could end up hitting with the wrong knuckles and break your hand.

- Orientation. Is he facing you or standing sideways? Or something in between the two of you? Is he standing right in front of you or slightly to your side? E.g. targets that are available when he is right in front of you become harder to hit if he takes a more bladed stance while standing more towards your side.

Play with these concepts to see how they interact and change how, when and where you hit.

Now let's look at the most reliable targets.

1) The chin

An effective way of creating a knockout is by rotating your opponent's head in a violent manner. There are different ways to do that, but perhaps the most effective is by landing a blow to the chin. Create a sudden acceleration of his head by striking the chin so it rotates his head to the side, upwards or at an angle. This can rattle his brain inside his skull and best-case scenario, knock him out.

2) Temple area

As the temple is a weaker area of the skull, blows landing there transfer their power more efficiently into the brain, causing a knockout or making him go all wobbly. The downside is that it is harder and less yielding than other parts of the human head, so you risk injuring your fist if you don't hit it correctly. If you miss, you're likely to hit a harder part of the skull, which increases the risk of injury even more.

3) The throat

Though illegal in sports boxing, I include this target because it easy to train for. You already target the chin in your regular boxing, so hitting the throat is not that much different. It is hard to do with a big boxing glove, but much easier with a bare fist. There are two ways to attack the throat: from the front and then from the side.

If your opponent is a man, from the front means you hit the Adam's apple. Though it is possible to "break" it, you're more likely to push it inwards and make him choke up for a little while, especially if you hit with bouncing impact. However, if you land a more powerful shot and cause structural damage, he might end up unable to breathe and eventually die. Proceed with extreme caution when selecting this target.

On the sides of the neck are arteries and nerve clusters that are vulnerable to impact. Landing a punch there, even a quick and fast one, can result in spectacular knockouts. Once again, the downside is obvious: if you hit too hard, you can actually kill somebody.

On general principle, attacking the throat and the side of the neck is not out of bounds in self-defense, but you need to have a good reason for it. Not every self-defense situation is life or death. Understand that if the police get involved, your actions have to hold up in court afterwards. It is safer to assume this will happen and that you're recorded on video. If the jury sees you repeatedly punching a guy in the side of the neck, you're likely to end up in prison. So, use good judgment and make sure you're legally justified when you go for this target.

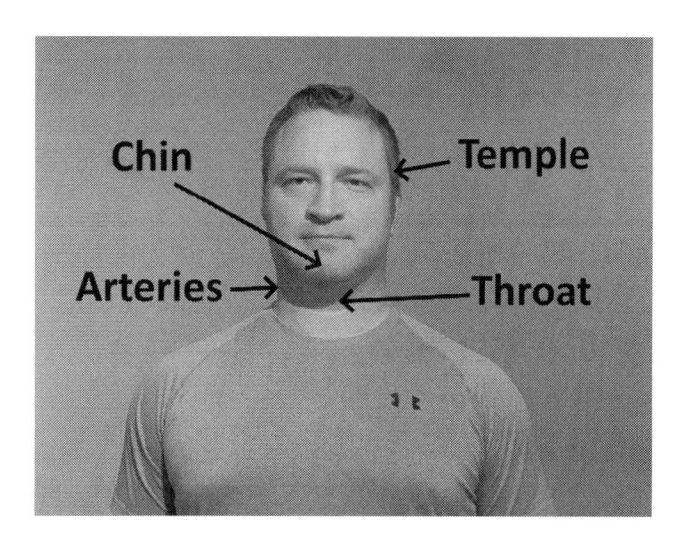

4) The diaphragm and solar plexus

The diaphragm is a muscle that separates your thoracic cavity from your abdominal cavity. It contracts as you inhale, increasing the volume of the thoracic cavity, meaning it lets you expand on the inside to let in more air. When it relaxes, the air flows back out.

The solar plexus is a popular name for the celiac plexus. It is a cluster of nerves that consists of several smaller plexi. "Plexus" is a Latin adjective that means "interwoven" or "intricate" and as a noun it can refer to a "braid." The best way to view the celiac plexus is as an interwoven network of arteries and nerves that help regulate several organs and bodily functions.

Both the diaphragm and the celiac plexus are located near the upper stomach, which is why I treat them as a single target.

When you get struck there hard enough, it feels as if you get the wind knocked out of you. Your diaphragm spasms and locks up your breathing. Until that spasm goes away, all you want to do is curl up in a foetal position and curse the day you were born. If the blow also messes with the celiac plexus, you're treated to some hardcore pain on top of that. Your organs are most likely undamaged, but it feels like they're massively malfunctioning, shutting down your ability to move, let alone fight.

The blow doesn't necessarily have to be spot on at the celiac plexus; if it lands near it and has sufficient force, it can still do the job. That makes it a relatively reliable target and you have a good chance of stopping your attacker immediately as their pain and inability to breathe leave him without much energy to attack you.

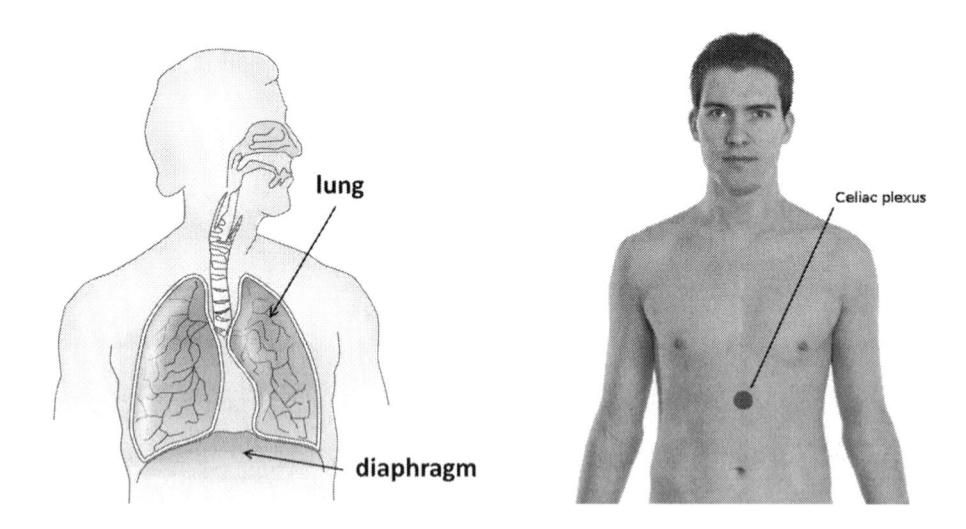

To successfully attack these two targets, you need two components:

First, enough power. I suggest a fragmenting or penetrating impact to hit deep enough into the target and cause the desired effect.

Second, if you miss and hit too high, your punch lands on his chest which is unlikely to cause much damage. If you miss low and hit him in the gut, this can have a similar effect than hitting the diaphragm but for different reasons. That said, be as precise as you possibly can. Train to land your punches where you want them to land.

5) The liver

The liver is situated on the right side of your body, slightly protected by the ribcage. It is one of the targets professional fighters like to go for in the ring, but it is much harder to consistently land a blow there in a self-defense situation. That is, unless you're a skilled and experienced boxer who can throw power shots without a warm-up, while still having excellent precision with your punches. The biggest risks are if you miss or only land a glancing blow, there is little to no result and the fight goes on. At worst, you end up in clinching range and it turns into a grappling match, which isn't your strong suit as a boxer. That is why I wouldn't advise going for it if you're just starting your training.

If you do want to attack the liver, make sure you hit with a penetrating impact that hurts him even if you hit a bit low or high.

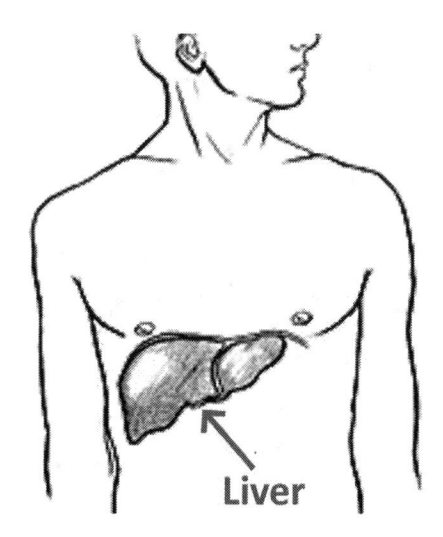

An important point about striking the body:

The saying in boxing is *"If you kill the body, the head will follow."* This means that if you land enough punches to the body, your opponent's head eventually comes down as well and he will fall. Though this is a successful strategy in the ring, I wouldn't recommend it outside of it. The reason is simple: you don't have time to build a victory like that.

Unless you pack a big punch or have excellent timing and targeting, it is the repetitive nature of body shots that puts your opponent down in the ring. Creating accumulated damage to the body takes time and effort. For self-defense, you don't have that time. That is why I suggest you look at attacking the body in a different way than you would in the ring:

- *Hitting the body is opportunistic.* If you see the opening for a solid body blow that does damage, take it, but don't overly focus on it either. Don't make it your only punch and don't expect it to finish the fight. It is just an opportunity to create additional damage or open him up to end it with a blow to another target.
- *Be precise to get maximum damage with just one punch.* My preferred target for attacking the body is the solar plexus/diaphragm. As I explained before, a good blow there shuts down the respiratory system and causes organ pain. He can't just try to endure the pain as his body simply doesn't function correctly anymore, making fighting you extremely difficult for him.

This is the kind of damage you want in a self-defense context: strike targets that have a high chance of achieving this goal. Don't go for targets that might be painful to receive a punch on, but your opponent can keep on fighting. In that light, I prefer to hit the diaphragm, and to a lesser degree the liver and lower ribs. Final targets are the bladder and the groin.

Some questions you might have:

Why didn't I include the groin as a target?

The groin is an illegal blow which I will cover along with other illegal blows in the second volume of this series on boxing for self-defense.

Why didn't I include the nose as a target?

I don't consider hitting the nose to cause enough damage to consistently stop the fight, even if you break it. I've had my nose broken with punches and kicks repeatedly and it never stopped me from continuing the fight. I've seen the same happen with others, it hurts and is annoying as hell, but you can almost always still fight. As a target, it isn't good enough for the streets.

Please go to wimdemeere.com/boxing for what is mentioned in this chapter.

Chapter Two: Getting started

Before you can get to the punching part, you need to master a few basics: have a proper fighting stance and know your footwork. These two allow you to not only throw hard shots, but also defend against them if your attacker throws first.

Without a good stance, you're easily off-balance, you can't generate a lot of power and you won't have good footwork.

Without good footwork, you become an easy target for a faster opponent, you can't close the gap when you need to, and you can get pinned up against a wall or other object because you can't get away in time.

A good boxer is comfortable in his fighting stance and can move around freely while maintaining his balance and control his body mechanics. This is just as important inside the ring as outside of it, though there are some differences between both arenas.

Let's delve a bit deeper into this.

Stance

There are key differences between a stance that works in a boxing ring and one that is useful in a self-defense situation. Here are the most important ones:

- You don't necessarily square off with your opponent. You have to fight from whatever stance you're in the moment punches start flying because you won't always get the time to drop into your fighting stance. Sometimes there might be a little bit of time to assume some sort of ready position, but don't assume this always happens. If he lands a sucker punch that knocks you off balance, you can only try to cover up and hope to get through the first couple seconds without getting knocked out. Anything goes in the street, and you should expect the unexpected.

A proper fighting stance is still useful once you're actually fighting, but you need the ability to flow into it from a different starting position. This never happens in the ring as the referee starts you off every time, so you have to train for it.

- A fighting stance can identify you as the aggressor in the eyes of the law. A boxing match is a sanctioned sporting context: two people enter the ring, under a set of rules, within an official organization, with officials making sure the rules are followed. The legal system has no issue with this.

  Once you step outside of the ring and square off with somebody, that is not automatically self-defense, as I explained in the previous chapter. When somebody gives you attitude and the first thing you do is square off with your fists, you might be branded as the instigator instead of the other guy. Depending on which country, state, and city you live, the law can take a variety of views on this, so make sure you research what your legal system is like before you need it. I listed some books in the resources page to help you with this.

- You might get caught on video. Nowadays, the odds of being captured on video are huge. CCTV cameras are everywhere, security systems capture your every move, or people simply use their cell phones to record the fight. Expect footage to go public, either by bystanders publishing it on social media or if you end up in court and the evidence is shared. This means your actions are recorded and interpreted *after* the fact. No matter how justified you feel in assuming a boxing stance, that looks very different from taking on what is called a "de-escalation stance." Again, we are talking about self-defense and not fighting, so you want to stack the legal odds in your favour as much as possible.

  You don't want to be seen as the guy who starts the fight; you want to be viewed as the person lawfully defending himself. How you act right before the first punch is thrown has a huge influence on the perception of witnesses and the actions of law enforcement afterwards.

Another reason is this:

The fight often only starts *after* you receive the first punch:

- You might be in a club when a brawl breaks out. You don't hear anything because of the loud music and your back was to the fighters before it started. The first thing you know that a fight started is when they slam into you from behind.

- You might be set up by a street thug who wants to rob you at the ATM. Let's assume you mess up and didn't pay enough attention to your surroundings. You don't spot him, and he clocks you over the back of the head.

In all these instances, you don't have the time to assume a fighting stance. You need to fight from whatever position you find yourself in. Sometimes that's a neutral stance, other times you might have the opportunity to position yourself into a slightly better position to either attack or defend. In all cases, you want the ability to flow into your boxing or fighting stance. That is the key to making it work: no matter how the fight begins, you know how to get to a proper stance as quickly as possible. Practice punching, footwork, and defense from a non-boxing stance, but your goal is never to stay in that stance and fight from there. It should always be a transition to your fighting stance.

This brings us to the final reason why It is so important that you not only practice boxing for self-defense from your boxing stance:

if you can avoid the fight at all, *you should*.

Just because some guy is in your face, that doesn't mean you have to oblige him and throw down. Remember the title of this book is "*Boxing for self-defense*". The title is not "*Boxing to be an asshole and beat up people in the street*", nor is it "*Boxing to pick fights whenever you feel like it.*" The term "self-defense" has a specific meaning, one you cannot ignore simply because somebody hurts your feelings, disrespects you or looks at you the wrong way. Bear all this in mind when reading this next part.

Let's take a typical example of an altercation:

You're somewhere in the street when a guy walks up to you and engages you verbally. He gets antsy and clearly tries to provoke you into a fight. If you assume a boxing stance, it is likely to create one of two situations: he backs down (perhaps cussing you out as he retreats), he says or does something to trigger you into throwing a punch or it escalates the conflict and *he* throws the first one.

Once again, assume you will be caught on video and the altercation is later analysed by police and lawyers if it goes to court. Self-defense is more than just surviving the violent encounter, it is also making sure you can afterwards return to your normal life instead of facing jail.

Look at this scenario again and consider that in the early stages of the confrontation you shouldn't be flat-footed and wide open for a sucker punch. But you also shouldn't necessarily be in a fighting stance. There is some middle ground in between, and I like to call this the ready-position or your de-escalation stance.

This stance has several goals:

- First, as much as possible, you want to be in a position that looks natural. When somebody else looks at you, they shouldn't notice that you're ready to defend yourself. On the other hand, it can also be a part of your de-escalation strategy. If the guy stepping up to you has some experience, he might notice the de-escalation stance and get the message you're sending him: *I don't want to fight but I'm ready if you even twitch.* In a number of cases, this is enough to make him decide to go pick on somebody else. If the opposite happens, at least you're ready.
- You won't always be able to assume a fighting stance. Sometimes you have to make do with whatever stance you find yourself in. However, that doesn't mean you shouldn't try to improve it, which is where the de-escalation stance comes into play. It not only gets you ready to act, it also allows you to verbally and nonverbally de-escalate the conflict. If that helps you avoid a fight, then that's just great. Nobody wins every single fight they get in, so the more fights you have, the higher the likelihood it ends badly for you.

View the de-escalation stance as an intermediary step between being flat-footed, totally unprepared to defend yourself, and dropping into your fighting stance, ready to throw down. Think of it as a scale of intensity where on the left side we have a perfectly natural stance that you assume when you're talking to friends, you stand relaxed with your arms hanging to your side. This leaves you wide open to a sucker punch, but as there is no danger, there is also no need to be ready for it.

A little bit more to the middle of the scale is a situation where there might be an issue, but you're not sure yet. Now you balance yourself on your feet, maybe slightly bend your knees, and pay attention to what's going on.

Moving along that line some more, now you're in a situation that can go haywire in an instant, but it is not quite there yet. You assume a de-escalation stance that gives you as many advantages as possible should it kick off, while also not provoking violence from the opposing party.

Finally, all the way to the right of the scale, we have your actual fighting stance. Only use this one when punches start flying. You use a fighting stance to fight, not to de-escalate, not to talk to the guy, not to convince anyone that you don't have violence in mind. Why? Because nobody will believe you when they see you with your fists held high, ready to strike.

Here are several everyday stances that can flow into a fighting stance:

1) First off, simply stand upright with your feet next to each other and your arms hanging relaxed by your side. This position leaves you completely open and vulnerable. You have no balance, it is hard to generate power and whatever your opponent does, it is difficult to defend against it. That doesn't mean you can't do anything from here, but the odds are not in your favor. Avoid such a stance when you spot a potential problem that risks escalating. People mess this up instinctively when their ego is engaged or they are emotionally involved, as opposed to focused on self-defense. You typically see two guys almost chest-to-chest, chin jutting out and feet planted flat next to each other in this neutral stance.

Not only are they way too close to each other and therefore at risk, they also have their hands down and aren't paying attention to anything other than the guy standing right in front of them. From that position, the first guy to attack usually wins the fight. At this close range, the average human reaction speed is not quick enough to do something about it.

Pretty please with sugar on top, *never* do this kind of thing. If you're the guy on the losing end, your tactics suck. If you throw the first punch, you're an asshole. Don't just knock people out because you're in a stupid argument with them. Act like an adult and walk away to sort it out later when you've both cooled down.

2) A slight improvement over this stance is what is sometimes called the "Jack Benny" stance. It refers to an old comedian who used this position in his act. Keep your feet where they are and fold your right arm in over your stomach, your left arm bends in with the forearm vertical. Place your fingers under your chin or touch your lips as if you're paying close attention to what somebody says. This protects your body a little bit and at the same time positions your arms close to an incoming attack. There is no guarantee you will react in time to a sudden attack, but you're at least better positioned to do so than before.

3) A variation of this one is the "clasped hands" one. Same neutral feet as before, but this time you put your hands on your stomach one hand on top of the other. Your elbows are slightly bent, and your chin is a little bit down. This has similar advantages to the Jack Benny stance but lends itself more to attacking an aggressor.

4) Use the exact same stance as here above but now lower your hands. You often see violence professionals use such a stance as it obviously makes it easier to protect the groin, but it also doesn't look threatening. They can still de-escalate the situation from there, but if it comes to blows, they are ready to act.

5) The next step is adding a slight angle to your foot placement. Use whatever stance from the list here above, but with one change: keep one foot slightly back.

If you fight from a left lead, Orthodox stance, place your right foot slightly back. This makes it easier to flow into your fighting stance and you also gain some stability. You can brace on that back leg a little to avoid being completely off balance should he charge in. It also still looks natural, though not as much when compared to the previous stances. But it's still nowhere close to an actual boxing stance.

6) Now we come to the "active de-escalation stance." Make your stance a little bit bigger by stepping further back with that right foot, but you're still not in a true fighting stance. Blade your body some more by pointing your lead shoulder forward and move your rear shoulder more to the back. Slightly move your elbows so your open hands point towards your aggressor, palms down.

This is almost universally accepted as a placating gesture and most witnesses interpret it as you're trying to calm things down. You can also make small pawing gestures: bring your hands up and down, clearly demonstrating you want to keep the other guy away from you. If the situation escalates you can still try to verbally de-escalate it, but you're already much closer to your fighting stance.

7) Finally, we get to your actual fighting stance. The moment to use it is when you get sucker punched and survive the first attack: orient on your attacker in this stance. Another option is when the guy makes a move and it fails to make contact and the fight is on.

This time make your step even a little bit bigger; your feet are far apart with your lead foot all the way forward and your rear foot back. Slightly bend your knees, tuck in your chin, bring your elbows in tight and keep your hands up. You can choose to make fists or keep your hands open, that's up to you.

These are all just examples and ideas for you to play with, they are not dogma. Find something that works for you by giving the ones listed above a try. Tweak them until they work best for the kind of situations you often encounter. Another good exercise is to visualize different contexts in which you would use them: if you're at a party at work, a soft de-escalation stance is more appropriate when a drunk colleague gets belligerent than immediately slipping into a fighting stance. On the other hand, if a junkie tries to mess with you in a store, standing in a neutral position with your arms down might not be the wisest course of action. It is not about which stance is best, but which one is appropriate for the situation. Train in all of them so you understand their individual benefits and limitations.

Train to throw punches from each individual stance. Practice how to set up straight, punches, hooks or uppercuts from each position you can find yourself in at a given point in time. After that first punch, figure out how you can drop into your fighting stance and either continue fighting or get to safety.

Try these two easy tips for best results:

- Imagine a bunch of different scenarios of how an altercation could start, how you would react to it and what the results would be. Adjust your stance accordingly.

- Study video footage of people fighting and see what happens right before the punches start flying. Notice how they stand, their weight distribution, where their hands are at which point in time, and so on. Use that information to improve your own training and implement what works for you. Go to the resources page for several such examples.

Footwork.

It doesn't matter how hard you can punch if you can't hit the target because it is out of reach. The only way to get close enough is with good footwork. Every boxer knows a flat-footed fighter doesn't get far in the ring. The same applies to self-defense, with some slight modifications.

First, let's look at the purpose of footwork: to get you in position to land your techniques and to make it difficult for your attacker to do the same.

The first part is simple; you want to get to the right position so you can throw whatever punch you need to use at that specific point in time:

- To stay at long-range, take a small step forward so you can throw a jab or cross, but not any closer than you need to reach the target. Don't overcommit by leaning forward.
- To come closer to your opponent, take one large step or two normal ones in rapid succession. As you close in, land a hook punch.

The same applies in a defensive context. if you don't want to engage your attacker, you need the skill to quickly move out of range. Or you might want to stay in range, but not in front of him. That's where pivoting and sidestepping comes into play.

All this means is that you need to move your feet.

We've all seen Mohammed Ali do his "Ali Shuffle" in the ring, and many more and boxers fought with similar fancy footwork with great success. There's absolutely nothing wrong with that in a boxing match. However, when it comes to self-defense this is not advisable, to put it mildly. One of the best ways to end a fight is to put somebody on the floor, and then stomp him, smash his head in with an improvised weapon or have some friends help with the stomping. The one thing that is necessary to get that done is to break your opponent's balance.

Loss of balance is always the precursor to a fall.

If you can unbalance your opponent and knock him on his ass, even if he isn't knocked out, he's very much at a disadvantage on the floor. The same applies to you though: if your footwork always puts you at risk of being off balance, you might end up on the floor and have one of those horrible scenarios happen to you. That is why you need to focus on solid, basic footwork that might not be all that flashy to watch, but it keeps you safe and gets the job done. Leave the fancy stuff to the wizards of the ring, who are paid to show that skill in high profile boxing matches. When it comes to self-defense, strong basics and sound fundamentals you can trust to work even under the most extreme stress are what you want. My take on footwork is relatively simple and basic but know you can rely on it when it counts.

Let's look at the basics: linear footwork.

- Forward step: start from your fighting stance and take a step forward with your lead foot, covering only a couple of inches. Drag your rear foot up the same amount of distance so your stance has the same length as it had before you stepped. Pay special attention to not lean forward or backward, don't move your hands up and down, and generally try to be as stable as you possibly can.

    Stepping forward engages your opponent as you step into striking distance or into the next range if you were already at long range. Stepping forward is offense.

- Backwards step: once again start from your fighting stance but this time step a few inches backwards with your rear foot. Transfer your weight together with your foot and then drag your lead foot along with you the same distance.

The backwards step gets you out of the way and is your default defensive manoeuvre: step out of range before he can counter you. This is a reliable tactic to get you clear and is relatively easy to pull off under stress. Don't stop there though. It gets you away from the initial attack but still leaves you in the line of fire of your opponent's weapons. Stepping back is therefore only a short-term solution.

Almost nobody can retreat faster in a straight line than an attacker can charge straight forward. If you want to test this theory, run 20 yards forward at your top speed, clock your time, and then compare it to how fast you can run 20 yards backwards. It is not even close. Humans are not meant to run backwards, that's not how our bodies work best.

Stepping back isn't useless and you should certainly practice it, but don't stop your skill development there. Add different follow-ups to that first step back by taking a second step back, getting to the side, pivoting, etc. This makes you a more elusive target and can slow down an aggressive attacker by forcing him to adjust to your footwork.

- Sidestep left: step 90° to the left with your lead foot and drag up your rear foot the same distance and direction. Practice this slow at first because it is a bit difficult at first to avoid overcommitting and losing your balance. This takes some practice and getting used to so don't worry if it doesn't work well right away.

- Sidestep right: this time step 90° to your right with your right foot. Then drag up your lead foot the same distance in the same direction. For many people, the sidestep right feels extremely uncomfortable. Once again this is perfectly normal as it is a bit awkward to step into that direction at first. However, with practice you get better at this so keep at it.

Stepping to the side is a versatile technique. I like to use it defensively by suddenly stepping to the left or right after landing a hard punch. While he recovers from that blow, my sidestep lets me escape to safety by denying him the chance to close in and clinch. For offense, it works great to keep attacking if he tries circle around you. Stepping to the side then lets you cut him off while at the same time keeping him in your line of fire.

- Shifting or full step. This is a relatively rare type of footwork in modern boxing, though it has slowly made a comeback thanks to fighters like Gennady Golovkin. This is old-school boxing footwork so you might feel awkward when you first try it.

Start from your fighting stance, but instead of stepping forward with your lead foot, now you step with your back foot. This means you effectively change from an Orthodox to a Southpaw stance.

There are two basic ways you can do this: the first is to pivot with the same side shoulder, so when you step forward with your right foot your right shoulder comes forward. This allows you to power a right-hand punch as you step. The other way is to twist your left shoulder forward as you step in with your right foot. This gives you a powerful left-hand punch when you take that full step.

Both versions are useful and which one you use depends on the specifics of the fight you find yourself in.

As this is footwork you rarely do in the ring, it takes some adjusting to manage a full step as opposed to the shuffling footwork boxing typically uses. However, in self-defense situations, this is often necessary. The surface you're on might not allow for shuffling footwork: you're in a bar with a wooden floor and spilt beer all over it, or on wet grass, or perhaps it's been snowing outside when you get attacked. There are lots of possibilities when you think about it.

The downside of the shifting step is that it's a bit telegraphed in comparison to regular boxing footwork. To overcome this slight disadvantage, initiate it with speed and commitment.

The upside is the massive power it generates through inertia: your whole bodyweight and mass moves forward and if you can connect a punch to that momentum, it becomes a tremendously heavy blow.

Next up is circular footwork. Use it to create angles and put yourself into a more advantageous position in relation to your opponent.

- Pivot left: take a small step to your left with your lead foot, then keep your weight on it as you pivot with your right leg in a semi-circle towards your left. The biggest challenge with this technique is staying in balance and stopping the motion when you want to. Pay special attention not to lean too far forward with your upper body as this brings your head in range for his punches.

- Pivot right. Take a step with your right foot towards your right at about a 90° angle. Then withdraw your left foot so you have the same distance between both feet again. This pivot is a bit more difficult to pull off as it feels like going off balance at first. The trick is to take a larger step than normal with your right foot so you can then retract your lead foot to your fighting stance. This larger step allows you to create some distance between you and your opponent as you create an angle.

An easy trick for both pivots and sidesteps: if you want to side-step or pivot to your left, throw your head a little bit in that direction as you initiate the footwork. Do the same thing when moving towards your right, lean your head a bit to the right as you initiate the footwork. Don't overdo it or you end up off-balance. It is an easy way to initiate the movement at first to get better at the coordination. Eventually, you no longer need it.

- Slide back left. This time were going to work on diagonal angles. From your fighting stance, step with your right foot as if you're going to pivot towards your left. Instead of making a 90° angle you stop at 45°. Make sure this is a large step so you can then retract your lead foot and maintain a normal distance between both your feet. You should face your opponent at a 45° angle the moment you stop the footwork.

- Slide back right. It is the same as the previous technique, but now pivot right with your right foot towards the 45°. Once again maintain the normal distance between both feet as you slide your left foot and end up at 45° towards your opponent.

These are basic footwork patterns boxers use in the ring. With just a few months of training, you should have no trouble using them outside of the ring as well. Don't view these different types of footwork as separate techniques, as they are meant to be used together. Practice going from one to the other in all possible combinations. The purpose of footwork is to give you the mobility to be at the exact spot where you need to be. It gives you freedom of movement, which in turn allows you to adapt on the fly depending on circumstances.

For instance, if you're always heavy on your lead foot, getting out of the way of an onrushing attacker becomes difficult. But if you're too light on your feet and always dancing around, you risk getting pushed or shoved off balance by an aggressive attacker. Instead, practice your footwork so you're always in a position to do whatever technique necessary, both for offense and defense.

The most important difference between footwork in the ring and the street is that flashy stuff is a bad idea. Dancing around like Muhammed Ali in a self-defense context often means you risk suddenly being off-balance. Or you end up on the floor because you slipped, overcommitted or your opponent pushed you off-balance as you were happily shuffling around him.

The second reason is that the longer the fight takes, the higher the chance of something going wrong or somebody intervening to your detriment. Instead of wasting time by dancing around, make your footwork clean, solid, dependable and functional. The goal is to allow you to strike your opponent at will, while making it hard for him to hit you back.

Drill

The key to making your boxing footwork functional for self-defense lies in the ability to change directions. This is true in sports boxing as well, but it's even more important from a self-defense perspective. You have to adjust the distance to your opponent, sometimes to multiple opponents, to obstacles that get in your way, and all other environmental factors that might cause problems. The ability to move quickly yet also instantly change directions is one of the most important skill sets you have to develop.

Develop this skill by spending some time on your footwork during each training session. I like to do so with footwork drills as a warm-up: after a general warm-up, I spent one or more rounds on simple or complex footwork drills. I change them rapidly and consistently after each session, to avoid getting stale or bored due to their repetitive nature. If you take a similar approach, you quickly advance with your footwork. With consistent practice it becomes crisp and controlled and therefore allows you to strike better.

A basic way to drill footwork goes like this:

- Start from your fighting stance and take one step forward.
- Step straight back.
- Sidestep left followed by a sidestep right.

- Pivot left and then right
- Slide step back to the left and then the right.
- Finish up with two forward shifting steps. First move forward with your right foot and then take another full step with your left so you practice both sides.

By doing the basics like this, one after the other, you quickly become more comfortable doing them, but you also practice changing directions. The pattern always sends you into a different direction than the one you just went: going from left to right, forward to backward and so on. This forces you to not only generate power to move your body, but also to control that movement and stop it in an instant. Then you immediately generate power again to reverse directions and go the other way or do the opposite movement from the one you just did. This in turn teaches you one of the most fundamental skill sets every combat athlete needs, regardless of which sport art he practices: **the ability to decelerate.**

Most practitioners spend an inordinate amount of time on accelerating their movements to become more explosive. This is a critical factor in developing good technique; you get no argument from me there. However, an equally important skill is the ability to stop your momentum and change directions. Instead of getting dragged off-balance by your punch when it lands or misses, you need the ability to retract it and flow into the next movement, whatever it may be. That ability is *deceleration*.

Suddenly and harshly stopping an explosive movement correctly takes time and practice. Sloppy fighters don't pay attention to this and leave themselves wide open because of it. They throw a powerful punch, but when it misses or glances off, their momentum drags them off-balance and forces them to step to regain their balance. Or they have to spend time recovering their balance before they can retract their punch and do something else. In the meantime, they are wide open as it takes time to regain balance. Time the opponent can fill with punching them in the face...

Deceleration is a critical factor in everything you do as a boxer. Not only in striking but most importantly with your footwork. That is why I prefer to drill this quality, over and over, to ingrain it. The same applies in self-defense: you want to step exactly where you need to be, without overcommitting or being forced to do additional movements afterwards to compensate.

The previous drill is basic and simple. Once you're comfortable with it, start mixing things up. There are different ways to do this:

- Reverse the order. Start with shifting steps, then going into the slides, then the pivots, followed by the side stepping and finally linear footwork. This feels awkward at first but keep practicing until you get the hang of it.

- Work in a predetermined geometric pattern. For instance, imagine a cross on the floor and keep your fighting stance centred on it in the middle. Try to follow the lines of the cross perfectly: step forward and back in a straight line. Next, sidestep perfectly along the other axis. Then you pivot to the left and right. Whatever you do, always end up on the lines of the cross.

- Once you can do the cross, try a square. This time you trace the square in different directions: start by stepping forward, then to the right, then back and finally to your left. If you dipped your lead foot in paint, it should have drawn a perfect square on the floor.

  Now repeat the drill in the opposite direction, going forward, left, back and then right. This forms a square in the opposite direction.

- Repeat the exercise but step back first. Then you go to the side, forward and again to the side. Do this in both directions.

- If you do all the previous "square" drills, you have four squares drawn on the floor with that imaginary paint on your lead foot.

- Add circles. Mix linear stepping with pivot steps, going from a straight line into a half circle. For instance, take a step forward, and then pivot 90° towards your left. Then take a step back, and pivot 90° to your right. Once you can do that comfortably, mix things up with side steps combined with the pivots or, do pivots first and then sidestepping or use the linear footwork forward and backwards any time in-between. Your goal is to mix it up as much as possible.

- Training tip: draw the patterns in chalk if you practice outside or use tape to make them inside the house. This visual representation makes the drill much more practical as it gives you clear directions on where to step.

The variations of this footwork drill are endless; you're only limited by your own imagination. In the examples I gave you only took a single step. You can also do double or triple steps with each type of footwork to make it more challenging. Or you can double up on one type of footwork, and do a single one of another, and then three repetitions of yet another type.

However, at the same time you want to remain in balance and be able to punch or defend both as you do the footwork, right before and right after stepping. If your footwork drags you off balance and you have to spend time stabilizing your body, then you're straying from what makes boxing effective for self-defense. Then you're dancing again, which is risky in the street.

Please go to wimdemeere.com/boxing for what is mentioned in this chapter.

Chapter Three: Basic offense

Jab

The jab is perhaps the most important technique in modern sports boxing. It is typically used to set up techniques, gauge distance and lead in longer combinations. The downside of the jab is that, even though it has lots of speed, it tends to lack the power you need to finish fights. It is rare to see an opponent get knocked out in the ring due to a jab and the same goes for the street. Below I share some options to remedy that, but first, here are some of the ways that anybody can use it:

1. **As a pre-emptive strike.** You're in a situation where you know that it will come to blows. You have tried to de-escalate things, but nothing works, and you don't have an easy exit. At that point, you can use the jab to surprise your opponent with a sudden and unexpected attack. If you land it correctly, it has enough force to stun him momentarily and buy you time to escape.

2. **In a quick combination.** Sometimes a single strike is not enough, and follow-up techniques are necessary. Imagine you're in a similar situation as in the previous point and need to throw a pre-emptive strike. However, you're facing a bigger and stronger opponent now. You know that a single jab is not enough to put him down. Instead, use it as a distraction to buy time to throw a more powerful technique, like a cross or a hook.

Here's how you do at basic jab:

- Stand in your fighting stance and keep your arms relaxed, but ready.
- Step forward with your lead foot and at the same time straighten your lead arm. Make sure to rotate your shoulders so they form a straight line with your lead arm. This increases both the range and the power of the technique.
- Tighten up your entire arm upon impact.
- Immediately step back with your lead leg as you retract your arm.

Some pointers:

- Watch out for hyperextending your elbow. The jab is a fast technique and it is easy to misjudge the range and then not have enough time to stop your punch. If that happens, you risk a violent lockout of your elbow and damage the joint. Avoid that by consciously practicing to only extend your elbow about 95% and then contracting the muscles in your arm on impact.
- Keep your chin down. Even experienced fighters make this mistake when they transition from the boxing ring to the street. Without thinking about it, they raise their chin, leaving them open to a counter. Instead, tuck your chin in and keep it protected behind the shoulder of your punching arm on one side and your non-striking hand on the other.

Watch a few boxing matches and look at how the fighters use their jab. In many cases they flick it out like a whip. This gives the punch a certain amount of pop, but it does not have devastating power. Given as they are not trying to end the fight in a handful of seconds, this is perfectly acceptable. In self-defense it is not, so we need to increase the power of the technique. Here are some options:

1. **Keep your elbow down.** To increase the power of your jab, keep your elbow aimed at the floor. This lets you more easily absorb the force of the impact when your fist connects to his face. It is guided through your forearm, into your elbow, to your shoulder and into your upper body, towards your legs, and finally into the ground. This puts a lot more mass behind your jab, increasing its power.

2. **Stiff jab.** Instead of whipping the jab out towards your opponent and then snapping it back again, contract your lead arm for a fraction of a second longer on impact. This turns it into what we call a stiff jab. By tightening your arm for just a handful of microseconds longer, more of your body mass goes into the punch, making it significantly more powerful. The downside is that it leaves you slightly vulnerable to counters, so retract quickly after the impact. Also cover up as much as possible during the punch to limit the danger.

3. **Drop step.** The famous champion Jack Dempsey popularized the drop step in his book "Championship Fighting: Explosive Punching and Aggressive Defense." It is a relatively simple technique, though it takes some practice to get the timing right. Here's how it goes:

- Stand in your fighting stance, your knees slightly bent.
- Without shifting your weight, pick up your lead leg. This immediately has the effect of making you fall forward.
- Recover your balance by stomping down on your lead foot, landing it an inch or two further in front of you than where it started from.

This is the basics you need to practice and ingrain to successfully use the drop step. It may feel awkward at first, but you quickly get used to it; just keep on training until you're comfortable doing it. Then, we can add techniques to it, starting with the jab:

- Once again assume a balanced fighting stance.
- Start the drop step by picking up your lead leg and letting your body fall forward.
- As you start falling forward, start throwing the jab.
- And now for the most important part: land the jab on the target *at the exact same time* your lead foot lands on the floor. This transfers your body weight that was moving forward because of the controlled fall, into the jab. The result is a jab a lot more powerful than the ones you often see in the ring.

As always, there are drawbacks. You have to train a long time to drop step correctly before you can pull it off in a self-defense situation. If you have been boxing as a sport, this takes some getting used to. Another downside is that it is difficult to get this coordination right when you're injured or just got sucker punched. Ingrain it well so you no longer have to think about it when you need it in real life.

Cross

Now it is time to bring out the big guns: the cross. In a regular fighting stance, the cross is your right straight punch. Because it comes from the rear, you can put more power into it by torqueing your entire body into it. Also, as it is a straight punch it travels the shortest path from your fighting stance to the target, making it a fast and effective technique with the potential to knock people out.

There is an additional benefit to using the cross in a self-defense situation:

In most street fights, you rarely see a well-executed linear strike. At best, the punch follows an oblique path, but it is more common to see whirling arms: people use punches to club their attacker over the head with, swing their fists around in circular or semi-circular trajectories and basically flail all over the place. As a result, it is often a matter of luck who lands the first blow and then goes on to "win" the fight.

Having the skill to perform a straight-line punch along centreline, right at the target, puts you several steps ahead of your opposition: your punch lands faster than theirs as it travels in a direct path to the target. An additional benefit is that you can also recover more quickly and strike again or even defend with the same arm. That is why I believe it is important to develop a good cross as a self-defense technique.

Here's how you do it:

- Stand in your fighting stance, your arms in a ready position.
- Use the closing rotation I explained in Chapter One. Drive of your back foot by lifting your heel, which will bend your back knee, rotate your right hip forward, torque your spine, and drive your right arm forward. All this in sequence creates a powerful punch. Don't forget to tighten your whole arm on impact to absorb the shockwave.
- Retract your arm by performing an opening rotation, torqueing the entire right side of your body back again so you resume your fighting stance.

Pointers:

- Don't lock out your elbow. Keep a slight bend in it to avoid hyperextension upon contact.
- Don't lean forward. It is instinctive to want to add power to the punch by leaning forward, throwing your whole body into it. Though this does deliver a more powerful strike, it also ensures you are off balance if the punch misses. This then leaves you wide open to get countered by your opponent. Instead, focus on good balance by keeping your spine upright and have some spring in your legs to help you control your centre of gravity.

Lead hook

Now that we covered the long-range techniques, let's look at what you can do when you're closer to your opponent: hook punches. At long-range you can straighten out your arms completely and deliver a lot of power that way. But if you're closer to him, you don't have the space to fully extend your elbows. The only real other option is to punch along a circular path instead of a linear one and land punches more along the side of the target as opposed to head-on.

Relatively speaking, hook punches are easier to do than straight-line punches. It is obviously still possible to mess them up so they lack power or you hurt yourself when throwing them. But the instinctive body mechanics of human beings are much more in line with circular punches than they are with straight ones.

Here's an easy example:

Ask one of your friends who doesn't practice martial arts or combat sports to participate in a quick experiment. Hold up a focus mitt with the striking surface turned to the inside, just like you would for catching a hook. Then ask him to slap the mitt as hard as he can, fully committing to the blow. You'll notice that he instinctively steps with his lead foot to then hit with his rear arm, rotating from the upper body, swinging the arm around in a circular trajectory so his hand hits the mitt coming in from the side.

These are the rough mechanics off the rear hook: with some minor tweaks, you can turn this slap into a right hook.

If you ask your friend to throw a right cross, the odds are good that he launches a looping punch or an overhand and ends up off-balance after he lands the shot, unlike with the slap. So most people don't have huge problems learning hook punches. It is the details that generate maximum power and keep you stable that are hard to learn, not the basic power generation or coordination.

All that said, here's how you practice the lead hook:

- Start from your fighting stance, making sure your lead forearm is vertical.
- Sharply pull your right shoulder back to generate power. This is a miniature version of the opening rotation. It is relatively hard to do at first, but with practice you can get better at it.
- As you rotate your shoulders, raise your left elbow until it is horizontal and at the same height as your fist. Doing so ensures your punch lands with the power of that rotation and then transfers it into the target via your fist.
- Resume your fighting stance.

Pointers:

- Don't rotate too much. If you turn too much into the hook, you expose your back. Don't forget that there's no referee on the street to separate you if he attacks you in the back. This is why I don't advocate transferring your weight onto your right leg or pivoting hard on the lead leg as you throw a lead hook. I know this is controversial and at first you might have difficulty generating a lot of power in your lead hook with these mechanics. But I believe that in the long run, it is a safer option and with practice, you can eventually make it a powerful punch.

- Thumb up or in? There are two basic ways of throwing a hook: rotate your fist so your palm faces you and your thumb points straight up. Or rotate your fists palm down, with your thumb pointing towards your upper body. There are pros and cons to both methods.

The thumb up version tends to be more stable and the odds of connecting with the right knuckles are relatively high. The downside is that twisting the wrists thumb up automatically tightens the biceps of your punching arm. As an experiment, throw the lead hook and keep your arm stationary at the end of the punch. Relax it as much as possible without lowering it and then first rotate your thumb all the way up and then all the way down. As you do so, look at your biceps and see how it contracts and relaxes during that rotation. This is basic anatomy and there's nothing wrong with it; it's just the way your biceps function.

Keeping your thumb pointing towards you with the palm of your hand facing straight down increases your risk of hitting with the wrong knuckles and breaking your hand that way. On the plus side, the punch tends to be a little bit faster and also easier to do from close range. It happens to be the version I prefer, but don't let that stop you. Practice both and see which one you like best.

Make a conscious choice to train a certain way, based upon your own experiences and experimentation. Don't just listen to dogmatic views from coaches and trainers, myself included. If there's one thing I've learned after 30 years of training, it's that not everything works for everybody all the time. What works for you may not work for me and vice versa. Hence the need for experimenting and creating variations of techniques that work specifically for you.

- Don't drop your rear hand. This is one of the most common mistakes beginners make: as they torque their right shoulder back, they also drop their right hand. The first reason why this is wrong is because it exposes that side of your face. Don't forget that you're standing close to your opponent, so he can easily counter you from that distance if you leave him an opening. The second reason is that it tends to wind up and telegraph whatever punch you might want to throw with that right hand after your lead hook. So keep that right arm tucked in tight and your right hand touching the right side of your face.

- Don't buckle your wrist. For proper power transfer, you want perfect alignment between your forearm and your fist. Not having that increases the risk of your wrist buckling on impact, possibly spraining it and most certainly weakening your punch. The easiest way to remedy this is lots of technical training, in particular during shadowboxing in which you pay attention to correct alignment. You want your elbow, forearm and fist to form a straight, horizontal line. That way, when the punch lands, you also minimize the risk of collapsing your wrist.

- Don't extend the elbow after you land. This is another common beginner mistake. When the fist hits the target, don't push it through by straightening out your elbow. This bleeds away the power, robbing it of its full potential. To avoid this mistake, focus on hitting a couple of inches into the target and then stop your punch instead of making your fist follow through.

Hook

You can hit extremely hard with the rear hook if you develop the proper body mechanics. Doing so isn't all that difficult because it shares many similarities with the cross that are transferable. Try it like this:

- Stand in your fighting stance and start the mechanics of a right cross.
- Instead of letting your arm shoot out straight in front of you, rotate your right elbow up so your fist travels inward in a circular trajectory.
- Hit the side of the target and then rotate your whole body back into your fighting stance, just like you did with the right cross.

Pointers:

- The same points apply as with the lead hook, with one addition: don't overcommit and turn the punch into a wild swing that breaks your balance. Practice retracting the punch just as much as you practice launching it at the target.

Lead uppercut

Another close-range technique is the uppercut, typically on an opponent who leans forward (exposing his face or chin) or against an opponent leaving an opening between his arms as he covers his head. Then you can throw a lead uppercut straight down the center so the punch lands in-between both of his arms.

In sports boxing this is fine but not in a self-defense context. When your attacker leans forward and is open to an uppercut, he also exposes the back of his head. This is a more vulnerable target that tends to yield more consistent results than the uppercut to the chin. There is a reason why blows to the back of the head are illegal in the ring: they work really well. But there are no rules in self-defense, so the back of the head is a better target to go for in such a situation. Opting for an uppercut instead is more difficult to perform accurately and will likely be less devastating.

A key self-defense principle is the tactic of "closest weapon to the closest target." If your opponent leans forward, then attack the back of the head (the closest target) with the closest weapon: a downward elbow, forearm, hammer fist or any of the other illegal blows. Tactically speaking, these are all better options than the uppercut and it's why I don't advocate spending lots of training time on the uppercut for self-defense. This doesn't mean there can never be a situation in which the uppercut is the best technique to throw; I know several "tricks" in which the uppercut can work very well. But there are better alternatives, in my opinion, and I will cover these in the second part of this book series. That said, for the sake of completeness, I include the uppercut here.

I teach the lead uppercut slightly different than in many boxing gyms. It is the way I teach beginners as I've noticed it often helps them understand proper body mechanics quicker. So give this method a try and if it doesn't work for you, do it the way your coach showed you.

- Start from your fighting stance. Make sure to keep your hands high and your elbows low.
- Slightly rotate your right shoulder forward as if you're throwing a right hook. Dip your left shoulder down a bit at the same time, but don't lower your hands.
- Do a sharp opening rotation and pull your right shoulder back. As you do so, drop your left fist a little and let it follow an upward, vertical trajectory towards the target. Twist your hips completely to generate lots of torque. As the punch connects, your fist needs to be fully rotated, with the palm of your hand facing you.
- Step back and recover to your fighting stance.

I've noticed through experience that this variation helps beginning practitioners quickly develop enough power to make their lead uppercut a dangerous weapon. By dipping your left shoulder as you rotate to set-up the lead uppercut, it is easier to twist your body in the opposite direction and generate tons of power. You can then make that forward rotation increasingly smaller, until it is almost imperceptible. But in the beginning, it is probably too complex to coordinate your body to develop sufficient torque with such a small movement. That's why I let students practice in largesse first, before showing them how to shrink the hip rotation down while still maintaining power.

Pointers:

- Don't pull your lead arm back as you rotate for the set-up. This is a classic mistake, especially with beginners or when you get tired, to load up the punch during the preparation phase. This telegraphs your intent and makes it easy for your opponent to counter. You're close to him for this punch so don't leave him any openings. Stay covered up and only let your fist go away from your face as it begins to strike.

- Don't make a backwards/forwards movement. As you set up by rotating your right shoulder forward, don't pull your arm back or down at the same time to load up. This is slightly different from what I mentioned in the previous bullet, in that it is no longer fully pulling backwards but more changing the trajectory of the punch. The trajectory of your fist should be a U-shaped curve as opposed to the straight line that the backwards/forwards movement generates. This is more along the lines of a straight punch.

A good uppercut follows a semi-circular path, starting by dipping your fist down and then rotating forwards to end up in a vertical ascent towards the target. This is one of the reasons why the lead uppercut is a difficult punch to master: you don't have a lot of hip rotation to generate power with. This instinctively makes many people *pull* their arm up instead of torqueing it upwards via the rotation of their torso.

- Don't pull the arm up. Though it is easy to develop this bad habit, generate power by torquing your body instead of using the deltoid muscle in the shoulder to pull up your fist. Sure, you still generate some power this way, but it is nothing compared to the devastating force of an uppercut that uses proper body mechanics.

- Don't buckle your wrist. When you're wearing boxing gloves and have your hands taped, this isn't as much of an issue because the equipment fixes your fists strongly on to your wrists. But when you're barehanded, maintain good alignment between your fist and wrists, keeping them on a straight line, so the wrist doesn't buckle on impact. That can lead to a sprained or even broken wrist.

Another similar and also common mistake is to flex your wrist slightly inward without thinking about it. This is an instinctive reaction as you contract your biceps to generate power. Misaligning your wrist like that is most likely going to damage it when your uppercut lands.

Uppercut

The rear uppercut mostly has the same tactical issues as the lead uppercut. Please refer to the previous text on the lead uppercut, as they are just as applicable here.

That said, the rear uppercut is a little bit easier to learn because you can use full body rotation now. If you miss the punch, or it doesn't have the desired effect, recovering is also a bit easier than with the lead uppercut. I consider it the "lesser of two evils" when it comes to uppercuts.

Here's how you can practice it:

- Start from your fighting stance again.
- Rotate the right side of your body forward as you did for the right cross and right hook, performing a closing rotation.
- As you rotate, slightly drop your right hand to start the forward movement in a semi-circular fashion, ending with your fist coming up vertically. Rotate your fist until your palm faces your body.
- Step back into your fighting stance.

Pointers:

- The same considerations apply here as with the lead uppercut. Please refer to those before practicing the rear uppercut.

Once more, let me stress that I have absolutely nothing against both the lead and rear uppercuts for self-defense purposes. I simply believe that if the opportunity is there to land an uppercut, more often than not, there is also the opportunity to throw more devastating attacks than uppercuts. This is one of those differences between sports fighting and self-defense fighting: what is an issue in one area is not even considered in the other.

I fully understand not all boxing coaches and self-defense specialists agree with me on that. As always, study and train in a way that works for *you*, and I will do the same. I share information and experience from my own perspective and hope that it can be useful for you. I make no claims that the way I teach is the only or even the best way. It is, however, what I know works and I feel confident in sharing it with you. As always, adapt whatever I write or say to your own specific needs and discard what you cannot use.

Resources page:

Please go to wimdemeere.com/boxing for what is mentioned in this chapter.

Chapter Four: Basic Defense

The point of boxing is to make sure you don't get hit while hitting the other guy. In modern sports boxing, the first half of this mindset is often sadly lacking. They just stand toe to toe and bang away at each other, seemingly oblivious to the fact that they are taking a lot of damage while trying to hurt their opponent. This strategy may work in the ring, but it is completely counterproductive for self-defense. There, your goal is never to draw out the fight or to take your time to finish your opponent. With every second the fight goes on, the odds of something going wrong for you increase. For example, while you're standing right in front of the guy, happily trading punches with him, his buddy cracks you over the head from behind with a beer bottle.

Always remember that for self-defense you want things to end *as quickly as possible* and your defense should reflect that mindset.

If the point isn't to drag things out, then what *should* the focus of defense be?

To answer this question, I'm going to take a page out of the book of one of the best boxers in history: Jack Dempsey. I mentioned his book "Championship Fighting" before, so I would advise you to read it because it is a treasure trove of solid information. Go to the resources page for a direct link to where you can get it.

A caveat: Dempsey's opinion on defense is consistently misquoted by people who should know better. This is despite him being exceedingly clear in his book and flat out saying so in the full title: "*Championship Fighting: Explosive Punching and Aggressive Defense.*" Many people interpreted his words to mean what has now become, in not only boxing but also self-defense circles: "the best defense is a great offense."

This is a strategic principle that has been used for a long time all over the world, and it most certainly applies to boxing as well. However, it is widely misunderstood to mean that attacking is *always* preferable over defending and Dempsey's words have been misinterpreted along these lines. Here's what he actually wrote in his book:

"You must have a good defense to be a well-rounded fighter and the best defense is an aggressive defense."

That is completely different than proposing to only attack during a fight. Dempsey specifically explained that each defensive technique should be done at the same time as a counterattack or should immediately be followed by a counterattack. In other words: make your opponent pay for attacking you by hitting him as soon as he throws a punch or right after, depending on which you can make happen first. This in no way, shape or form means you should neglect your defense to benefit your offense. It means that you are always on the offensive, even if you don't strike first, because there are fundamentally only two timing moments when you fight:

- You take the initiative and strike first.
- Your opponent takes the initiative and you immediately take it away from him by striking back at him.

That is what it means to have an aggressive defense: *always* try to hit your opponent, no matter what. At the same time, you want to avoid getting hit and that is where your defensive techniques come into play. What Dempsey meant is that you see each defensive technique as an opportunity to hit your opponent. Don't defend *just* to defend but counterattack your opponent. Your defense is *actively aggressive* as opposed to *passive*.

In the ring you can tire your opponent out by pulling him into later rounds of a 12-round fight, in the hope that his fatigue gives you the opportunity to beat him. But when you're fighting for your life, every second counts. Your strategy and tactics, including your defensive tactics, need to incorporate this sense of urgency: end it as quickly as possible. If you must defend, use it as an opportunity to try and put him down and out.

There are two ways to look at defense: active and passive. Let's start with the latter.

Passive defense means placing obstructions in your opponent's way and thereby denying him openings to certain targets.

For instance, when you throw a right hook, don't drop your left hand. This common mistake leaves you wide open to a counter hook on your left side. With regular training you can ingrain the habit of keeping your left hand high to protect that side of your face. Do this consistently for all your punches:

the non-striking arm should be in a defensive position where it has the most potential to protect you and is also in a position to attack immediately. Typically, this means keeping that hand close to the side of your face and your elbow and forearm close to your ribs.

Why is this important?

I have a theory which you can check each time you watch a boxing match:

Some openings are unavoidable; others are yours to give away.

For instance, the lead side of your body is open to counters if you throw the jab. If you opponent has good timing and speed, you can't stop him from hitting you there: opening up that lead side of your body is unavoidable because you need to straighten out your punching arm to throw that jab.

The same applies to all other techniques: there is always an opening somewhere and if you're unlucky, that's where your opponent strikes. However, taking the example of the jab again, you don't have to move your rear hand away from your face or your rear arm away from your ribs. It is well within your power to protect that side during the punch. Not doing so means you give your opponent an opening he did not earn. You gave it to him for free.

It is my contention that in the ring, more punches score a knockout or knock down through openings that were given as opposed to unavoidable ones. The reason why is that we are not machines, we make mistakes, especially when we get tired:

- We drop our guard, our opponent spots it and nails us for it.
- We load up on a power punch by retracting the arm before throwing it, leaving our head wide open.
- As we retract a punch, we drop our hands instead of bringing them straight back to protect our face.

The list goes on, but you get the point: we make mistakes, we leave openings we shouldn't. Once we are hurt, dazed, or tired, that's when these mistakes happen the most but also for two other reasons:

- Fighters are arrogant and think they have such good defense they can't be touched.
- We don't ingrain passive defense into our techniques from the get-go.

I believe passive defense is one of the easiest ways to make sure you don't get hit. It is also the reason why I emphasize this in the striking drills I make beginning students do. One of the first things they hear from me is "defense before, during *and* after you attack." There is no reason to view attack and defense as separate skills. They work best when you mix them together. Remember that the goal is to not get hit so you should do everything you can to avoid it. Also remember that even though you might be able to take a fair amount of damage when you're wearing heavy boxing gloves, things are radically different in a self-defense context. Soaking up damage is not a winning strategy there.

All that to say this: make sure your passive defense is always on point if you want to survive on the street. It might not stop everything your attacker throws at you, but it is in an additional layer of defense that does its part in keeping you safe. It can't do that if it isn't there.

High closed guard

This is the easiest and most instinctive way a beginning boxer blocks incoming punches. Raise both arms in front of you, elbows pointing forward and your hands in front of your forehead. This effectively creates a "wall" in front of the most vulnerable target, your head. As defensive techniques go, this is crude but effective. The opponent's punches crash into the guard instead of landing, but you still absorb a fair amount of each impact. Another downside is that you are vulnerable to the body as your arms are too high to protect against those shots. That is why this kind of guard is only used sparingly in professional boxing matches. You typically see it when a boxer is hurt or too tired to use other, more effective and safer defensive manoeuvres.

In large part, the big boxing gloves are what keep you safe. The padding absorbs most of the incoming strikes. Even though the impact still travels through to a certain degree, the high closed guard is better than getting punched full in the face.

For self-defense situations, this defensive guard needs to be adapted because you will not be wearing boxing gloves then. Here's how you can pull that off:

- Start from your regular fighting stance and imagine an opponent throwing a barrage of punches at your face.
- Rotate the right side of your body slightly forward so you can place both forearms in front of your face. Bring them as close together as possible. Because you aren't wearing gloves, raise

your elbows high enough so you can touch the back of your head with the palms of your hands. At the same time, shrug your chin down into your chest.

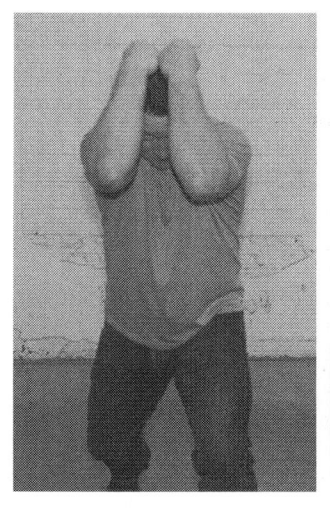

- Imagine the attack is over and your opponent retreats. In response, lower your arms while you rotate your right shoulder back again and resume your fighting stance. Don't drop your hands low because it exposes your face again. It is a common mistake, so practice avoiding it.

Some pointers:

- This guard is passive. Punch after punch slams into your arms and you just take it. You don't actively deflect, stop, or make your opponent miss his techniques. There really isn't anything to stop him from continuing to hit you. All this time, you take damage: your arms cannot keep absorbing the punishment and eventually your guard will open. When that happens, your immediate future looks bleak. Instead of overly relying on the high closed guard, use it as an emergency defense for when everything else fails. Train to instinctively work to get to a better position or re-take the initiative and attack back each time you use it. As I've written before, you don't want to be a purely defensive fighter.

To put this into another perspective, here's a quote from one of the most brilliant World War II military minds, Field Marshal Erich von Manstein:

"Now it is generally recognized that defense is the stronger of the two forms of fighting. This is only true, however, when the defense is so efficacious that the attacker bleeds to death when assaulting the defender's positions."

Heed this advice when it comes to the high close guard: it cannot protect you forever, so get out of it as soon as you safely can. Then take the fight to your attacker or run to safety. Whatever you do, don't just stand there taking a beating until he breaks through your guard.

- Palms down. Lack of gloves means you have to bring your elbows up higher, to not only have a more stable structure protecting your face, but also to put your hands out of harm's way. The human hand is made up of many small bones, weak muscles, and fragile tendons. When your hands almost touch the back of your head, they are out of reach of your attacker's punches. With a bit of luck, you can avoid taking damage to your hands and use them to strike back. Should he injure or break your hands because you kept them in front of your face, your offensive capabilities drop tremendously.

- Get small. Make yourself as small as possible behind your forearms. The tighter you keep your closed guard and the more you shrug down your chin, the less chance he has to sneak a punch through. This is another one of those differences between sports boxing and self-defense: in the ring 10 or 12-ounce gloves make your fist too big to sneak through that guard. In the street against a bareknuckle aggressor, he can sneak through relatively small openings and land a shot. So curl up tight as much as you can.

Blocking

In the ring, you can block circular attacks relatively easy, in part because you have big gloves that cushion a portion of the impact. As the glove is relatively large, you don't have to raise your arm all that high to still get a good block. In a self-defense context you don't have that glove, so you have to modify your blocking techniques slightly.

Another factor is that there are limits to using a block for self-defense. Unlike in the ring, in the street attackers can use weapons to beat you, rob you, or worse. In addition to that, smart attackers (and most experienced attackers tend to be at least street-smart) don't display the weapon until they use it. What looks like a sloppy haymaker punch to you might be a knife slash aimed at your throat. You can block such an attack by bringing up your arm like you would in the ring, but there is a huge difference between absorbing a punch on your block and letting a sharp, metal blade cut chunks out of your forearm.

The same applies when your opponent uses some sort of strike enhancer like brass knuckles, wears several heavy rings specifically for this purpose, wields some sort of tool like a small hammer or a wrench, etc. In these cases, simply taking the attack on your block is a recipe for disaster at worst and an injury at best. A traditional boxing block is not designed to handle that kind of punishment. On the contrary, its purpose is to absorb blows from opponents about your weight, wearing the same type of boxing gloves as you.

Keep all that in mind when you practice blocking. Assume you will never see the weapon until it is used against you. Don't simply dismiss this issue because even though not every single attacker you might face will be armed, it is safer to train as if he will be.

This is one of the biggest fallacies combat sports practitioners struggle with to effectively use their skills for self-defense.

The context is so radically different that they only look at the similarities and not the differences. So they don't train for those differences and don't adapt their techniques to this new context. It is easy to fool yourself, especially if you're a good boxer in the ring, to think that you would change and adapt your techniques on the fly when you notice your attacker has a weapon. Any boxer should know this is nonsense as the same adage that is used in boxing "you fight the way you train" is as true in the street as it is in the ring. If you never train to defend against knives and other weapons, it is naive to expect that you can pull a rabbit out of your hat and do so under extreme duress. That is simply not realistic.

Use the same logic you use to prepare for a fight in the ring: train as if it is going to be the worst fight of your life and the cards are stacked against you. If a less severe scenario materializes, then that's a lucky break. But instead of hoping for luck to come your way, assume the worst and train accordingly.

Here's how you can practice your blocking techniques:

- From your fighting stance, imagine a hook punch coming in from your left.
- Slightly bend your knees to better absorb the blow as you raise your lead arm. Bend your elbow as you bring it up and place your hand at the back of your head. Remember that you don't have gloves to protect you, so you need to use the structure of the entire arm to hide behind.
- Bring down your arm to your fighting stance afterward. Don't drop your hands lower than you normally would in your fighting stance.

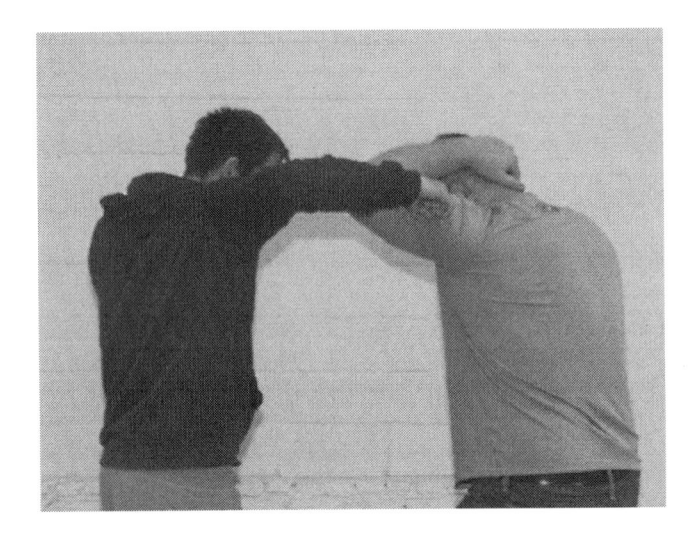

- Start again from your fighting stance. This time picture a hook punch coming from your right side.
- Use a small closing rotation to bring your right shoulder forward a little bit as you slightly bend your knees.
- As you do this, raise your right elbow (while keeping it bent) with your hand reaching around to the back of your head.
- Retract your right arm to your fighting stance, while simultaneously performing an opening rotation and turning your shoulders back into their normal position.

These are the two fundamental blocks for self-defense. They are slight variations on how you block in the ring and might feel somewhat uncomfortable at first. That is one of the reasons why I mentioned that training boxing for self-defense influences your ring-fighting skills. If you block like this in the ring, your opponent can nail you with shots to the body. Because that's where you are vulnerable when you raise your elbows higher than you normally would to block a hook. It is difficult to train for both the ring and self-defense at the same time because certain techniques are not compatible with the other environment.

Pointers:

- Don't pull down your opposite hand. It is an instinctive thing to do when you block, especially when this kind of technique is new to you. For instance, you block a short hook with your right arm, but this instinctively triggers a retracting motion with the left arm which pulls your left fist under your chin. This leaves you wide open on that side and your opponent can easily land a second punch there. The same applies at longer range when blocking typical street attacks like big haymakers. If there's an opening to be exploited, on purpose or by accident, you're vulnerable to attacks from your opponent. Make sure to keep your non-blocking side covered by holding your fist in position instead of dropping it.

- Don't lock out your legs. Even though your upper body does most of the work, your legs also play an important role. As you absorb the shock of the incoming strike, have some spring in your knees. That way the shock is transferred from your upper body through your waist, down your legs and into your feet. If you have stiff legs, you're likely to be knocked off balance due to the impact. If that happens, his follow up strikes have an easier time landing. Don't give your opponent such a free lunch and work on stability under stress. Practice blocking several punches in a row without losing balance. This develops your skill to the point where you can block full power blows without losing your balance. Remember that there is no referee to pause the fight if you fall in the street; balance matters.

- Find the sweet spot. Everybody is built differently and has a different body. Some people are thin with wide shoulders and long arms; others are of the stockier build. This all influences how you can block, and you have to figure out just how much of a bent you need in your elbows, and exactly how high you have to bring them to get a decent block. There is no one size fits all solution. The only thing you can do is practice and try different variations until you find what works best for you.

The previous defensive techniques were passive, but the following ones are not. I consider them active defense because they do more than just get in the way of the incoming attack. In fact, they take impact out of the equation by actively redirecting the attack or moving the target out of its path. This takes better timing and control than merely blocking, which means being more active.

Parrying

Parrying has a different goal than blocking: instead of *stopping* the punch to absorb the impact, you aim to *divert it away* from its target. Picture a punch coming straight at you and you slightly tap it to the side with your hand. That parry directs it a few degrees away from you, making it miss. The advantage is that it doesn't cost you a lot of energy while also making your opponent miss. Not only does this force him to expend additional energy to recover his technique, he might also end up overcommitting and lose his balance. That in turn offers you a perfect opportunity to counter him. Both these factors make parries excellent defensive techniques for ring-fighting.

However, I believe that parrying has only limited value for self-defense. Once again, I understand this is seen as heresy by many boxing fans and coaches, but there is once more the difference between the ring and the street: it is rare to see somebody perform a clean, straight-line punch in a street fight. It is much more common to see looping punches, hook punches, big haymakers, and other sorts of angled techniques, than encountering a perfectly placed, crisp jab or a cross. It does happen occasionally, but it's rarer than you might think.

First, because not many people are trained boxers. Second, even trained fighters mess up their techniques when they are under the stress of a real fight. It is one thing to perform under the pressure of a prizefight in the ring, with the referee and your corner to stop the fight if you run into trouble. It is quite another to suddenly be faced with a criminal trying to kill you for your wallet, when you least expect it and aren't warmed up. Even though you might be well trained, this different context and the surprise of the attack can make your brain short-circuit and not give you access to the skills and experience you developed in the ring.

As always, anything can happen where violence is concerned. However, we then come back to the adage of "you fight the way you train", so we must look at what is most likely to happen in a violent encounter. In my experience and as far as I can see from researching the issue, straight-line punches are much less common than other kinds. That is why I believe it is less critical for you to practice parrying techniques as a basic defense, than blocking or other options. However, I want to be thorough in this book, so I add them to here too.

Try this:

- Start from your fighting stance and imagine a jab coming at you in a straight line, right at your face.
- Move the palm of your right hand horizontally to your left to divert that jab away from your head.
- Immediately bring your hand back to your on-guard position.
- Now imagine your attacker throwing a cross.
- Move the palm of your left hand horizontally to your right to divert that cross away from its target.

Pointers:

- The parry needs to be fast to work correctly, so do it with snap.
- Don't catch the punch in the palm of your hand. The goal is to divert it, not stop it cold.
- Don't parry down as that only directs his punch towards a lower target. Though it is arguably easier to take a punch to the body than to the head, you still get hit.
- Don't overextend the parry. All you need is make him miss your face by a few inches, not half a foot. Reaching too far with your parry leaves you open to other attacks as it takes a relatively long time to retract your parrying hand so you can use it again to strike.

Spend some time training these parries, but not at the expense of other defensive techniques you are more likely to need should real-world violence come your way.

Head movement

Head movement is also extremely common in sports boxing, but it needs to be looked at through the lens of a self-defense situation. Boxers routinely slip punches in the ring to avoid getting hit, but they don't always counter from there. In the street, that is a problem. It isn't realistic to expect you can slip every single punch. Each time you give your attacker a chance to hit again, the odds of him landing on you increase. If you do evade the punch and don't immediately stop him, he can crash into you and start clinching, grappling, biting, eye gouging or take you to the ground. If he hits you with a sucker punch, the odds of you successfully using head movement while your brain is still scrambled are not good. In all these examples, the strategy of slipping a punch to reposition yourself for your own attack is often (though not always) counterproductive.

You don't have 12 rounds to construct a victory from scratch by slipping his punches, so he gets tired and becomes easy to pick off. Instead, end it as quickly as possible.

So how do you use head movement then?

Always do it in such a way so you can immediately counter your opponent.

Don't waste the opportunity you created by making him miss by doing something that prolongs the encounter. Instead, *attack him immediately*. Only let him get away unscathed with a missed punch when you truly have no other choice. To achieve this result, always think offense whenever you use head movement. Use it to set up your next shot instead of remaining passive afterwards.

Another use for head movement is as a reflex action to save you when somebody tries to hit you unexpectedly. This is sometimes called the flinch response or the startle response. It is an instinctive reaction innate in all human beings. Slipping a punch is essentially a more stylized and streamlined version of the startle response.

To see the startle response in action, sneak up on your cat or dog, and make a loud noise. You'll see what a startle reaction looks like (and also incur the wrath of your pet) in no uncertain terms.

Human beings have a similar response hardwired into our brains. The part of the brain that regulates this response is a primitive one that developed throughout the millennia. It doesn't do so well with logical thought, but it is very good at reacting quickly to sudden danger.

With some people and in some instances, the startle response is to move the head. It doesn't matter which way their head moves; what matters is that this response is instinctive and happens without conscious thought. This is why slipping punches can be such an effective move. It uses an instinctive movement innate to human beings and transforms it into a similar, more controlled movement that also allows you to immediately strike back upon completion. It is this last part that we want to train for self-defense.

Practice slipping punches like this:

- Start in your fighting stance as usual and imagine somebody jabs at your face.

- Bend your knees a little and lean slightly to the right with your torso as you snap your head to your right side.
- Don't exaggerate these movements so you're off balance, but also don't make them too small so you don't fully dodge the incoming blow. It takes some experimenting to figure out exactly how much you should move.
- As soon as you successfully slipped the incoming punch, stop the movement of your body instantaneously and immediately snap back up to your fighting stance. Keep your balance during this movement too.

Repeat this exercise but now imagine a jab or a cross coming at you and you want to slip to your left:

- Bend your knees again, but this time lean your body over to your left side as you snap your head away from the incoming punch.
- Freeze all movement in an instant after the punch misses and then reverse direction, snapping your body upright into your fighting stance.

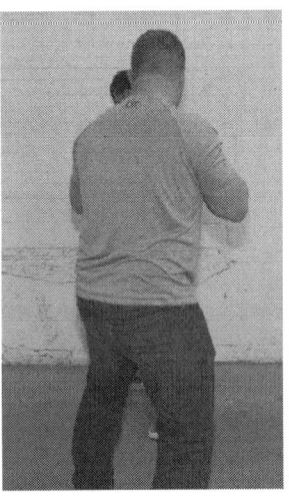

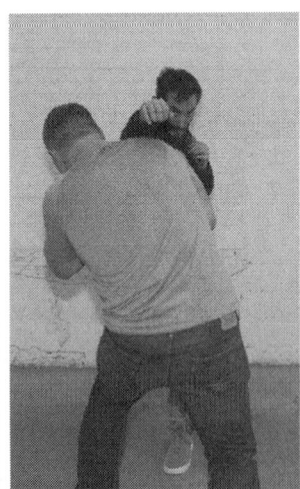

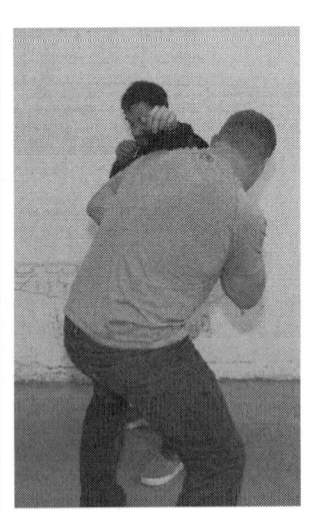

Pointers:

- Don't overdo it. If you launch yourself away from the incoming attack with such force that you're off-balance, then you miss your opportunity to counter. You also give your attacker another chance to strike. Make sure you get up immediately into your fighting stance as soon as he misses the punch.

- Snap back up right away. Though it is technically possible to stay in that leaning position as you slip his punch and fight from there, it is dangerous in a self-defense context. The biggest risk is that you get grabbed into a clinch or shoved off balance, either by accident or on purpose.
- Don't jump up. Beginners often make this mistake: they do a good job slipping the punch, but then get back to an upright position by straightening their knees too explosively. This lifts their center of gravity and breaks their balance. As you know by now, you don't want to lose your balance in a self-defense situation.
- As you practice, always remember that your goal is not *just* to slip the punch, but also to *hit back* as quickly as you possibly can. You want the fight to be over as soon as possible, so each time you make him miss, counter with a punch or combination of your own. That doesn't mean there won't ever be instances when you cannot counter after slipping his attack, but you should strive to make it so. End the fight as soon as you can.

Please go to wimdemeere.com/boxing for what is mentioned in this chapter.

Chapter Five: Basic Clinching

Wrestling-type clinches are not allowed in sports boxing, but they happen regularly in the street. People throw punches from either too close and clinch instinctively or they punch from too far out, overcommit and crash into their opponent. It should be self-explanatory boxers don't want to be in this type of situation, but to be clear:

Boxing's best weapons are punches, *not* clinching or grappling.

That is why in this section on clinching I don't focus on grappling per se, but more on how to avoid this range, while using techniques and mechanics from boxing. That doesn't mean I view grappling as useless for self-defense, on the contrary. However, the focus of this book is boxing techniques so going into too much detail about grappling is beyond the scope.

Here's another factor to consider:

Grabbing and holding while striking isn't allowed in the ring, but boxers routinely clinch by tying up their opponents to stop them from punching. They use the same tactic to rest or recover from a hard shot. The referee then pauses the fight, and both boxers have to take a step back before they start again.

In self-defense, *there are no such rules.*

This brings us to four major issues you need to adjust for when it comes to the clinch:

1) There are no clean breaks.

An aggressor can hit you as you get out of the clinch or when he lets go first. Expect this to happen and adjust your mindset and tactics accordingly.

2) At close range, you're likely to get grabbed and hit at the same time.

Holding and striking is an instinctive tactic many people use in real fights. One of the most common scenarios in a street fight is this: two guys flail at each other, one or both guys lose balance and they collide. This triggers an instinctive grabbing reflex which results in a clinch. That usually doesn't stop them from trying to land punches though. We can argue over the effectiveness, but these techniques are at the very least distracting if you aren't used to them.

3) In the clinch, your attacker can throw or trip you and you end up on the ground.

Over a century ago, throwing and grappling were often taught as a part of the sport, but modern boxing has completely outlawed such techniques. Today's boxers don't learn these and therefore don't practice how to defend against being taken down.

If you do end up on the ground, all your punching technique goes out the window and you're in another realm one you never train for, so don't expect to do well there. As a boxer, avoid it at all cost.

4) Outside of the ring, an attacker has many more tools at his disposal.

Your opponent can put you in a head lock, headbutt, bite, spit in your face, claw at your eyes, throw (even if not very effective) punches while holding on to you or slam/push you into a wall. He can also pull a knife or another weapon and try to kill you. All this is strictly forbidden in the ring and is never addressed in the training of a competitive boxer.

Does this mean that as a modern boxer, your techniques can't work in a self-defense situation in the clinch?

Of course not!

But you would be a fool to think the differences between clinching in the ring and in the street can't influence your effectiveness. As always, remember the old boxing adage "you fight the way you train." This means you have to adapt to this kind of clinching and develop a radically different approach from how you do so in the ring. To get you started, here is a drill you can do with a partner.

Discovery drill:

The goal of this drill is to discover which parts of the clinch translate from the ring to the street. Some techniques can still work for you, others not at all. Still others might need some tweaks and adaptations. The idea is to put yourself in situations where you can test all this out. Start *slow* and *gradually* crank up the intensity as much as safety allows. Wear bag gloves or MMA gloves for when you accidentally make harder contact than intended. Your partner should wear a cup and head gear.

This is a gradual drill in which you go to the next step *only* after you can comfortably do the previous one. Start with the first one and work your way up to the last one:

1. Practice getting used to a clinch where your partner holds you in various ways and doesn't let go. He uses one or two hands to grab your neck, arm, wrist and any part of your clothing. Try to punch from that kind of clinch.
2. Now try to break free from his grip so you can punch. Your partner must let you punch as soon as you're free.
3. Your partner can now immediately grab again when you break free. See if you can still punch then.
4. He can try to break your balance by tripping and throwing you. See how well you can punch then.
5. Now he tries to push you into (or over) objects like walls, furniture, etc. Stop him, break free and punch. Start very slow with this and obviously don't do this drill in your living room. Find a suitable place and get some free or cheap furniture you can trash.

Don't turn this drill into a fight or a hard sparring session; you don't learn anything if you end up in the hospital. The goal is to feel out techniques and get comfortable with a clinch that is oriented towards self-defense as opposed to ring fighting. Have a third person monitoring the drill so they can step in if it gets out of hand. When you or your partner end up in a bad position and the other doesn't realize it, this person can also prevent accidental injuries.

You get a much clearer picture of how clinching for the street works after only a few sessions with this drill. With that information, you can tweak and finetune your techniques so that they are effective outside of the ring as well.

You also discover most of the common clinch positions you can encounter in a street fight. In the rest of this chapter, I use terminology from the grappling arts to describe them, but don't focus too much on those names. It's rare in real fight to see perfectly executed, highly technical Brazilian jiu jitsu or wrestling techniques. However, the basic positions are the same, so we can work from there and then experiment with variations. Let's start with the first and most instinctive one.

High clinch or double neck tie

Grab control of your attacker by placing both hands on the back of his head. Keep your elbows bent so you create a hook with your hands and make sure your forearms are in front of his chest. Don't interlock your fingers.

There are several possible hand positions, but try these two first:

- First, place both of your hands on top of each other as you cup the back of his head with your bottom hand. Curl in your wrists to pull his head in tight.
- In the second position, your palms face each other instead of being on top of each other. Place them on each side of his neck and keep your elbows down as much as you can.
- Both hand positions work, do the one you like best.
- Once you get this grip, you can pull him down to break his balance or hit him with uppercuts and body shots as he is bent over.

Pointers:

- The biggest danger when an attacker grabs you in this clinch is that he can knee you in the face, which is an extremely powerful attack. His knee goes up and collides with your head as he pulls it down or he holds you down and throws multiple knees to your head that do cumulative damage. One good knee to the face can knock you out, so avoid ending up there at all cost.

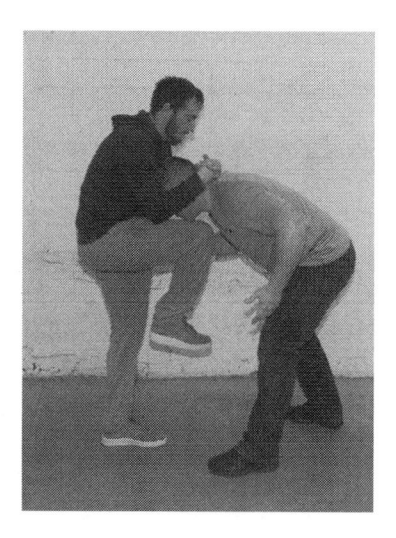

- Don't let yourself be pulled down, unless you're an experienced grappler. Even then it's risky because he can use his full bodyweight to break your balance. He can also make it difficult for you to generate power in your punches by yanking you in different directions. All that makes it a bad place to be in. Try to get out of it as quickly as possible.

Defense:

- To get out of this grip, push your hand on his opposite hip: your left hand pushes his right hip away or vice versa. Often, your lead arm is the quickest and easiest one to use for this technique. By pushing his hips back, you make it impossible for him to knee you hard in the face. It also gives him less leverage to manipulate your body while he's holding on to your head.
- With your other hand, shove one of his arms over your head so he loses a part of his grip and with some luck, you can get clear. Don't expect this to be easy; you'll probably have to fight your way out of that clinch with a variety of punches.

- As you fight to get away, remember that just because it is easy for him to knee you in the face, that doesn't mean he has no other options. He can also throw short uppercuts, elbows or hammer strikes to the back of your head. All illegal techniques in a boxing ring, but you should expect them in the street. So don't focus too much on one way of defending against this clinch.

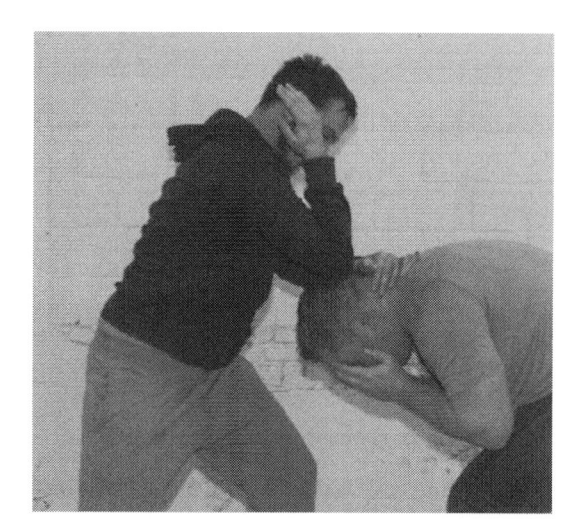

- If your opponent keeps you in-close, the defense is a bit different. You now don't have enough space for boxing techniques so focus on some dirty grappling instead:

Immediately grab his face and try to get your fingers into his eyes. Depending on how severe the situation is, you might need to dig into his eyes to make him let go. Many people instinctively protect their eyes then and either let go to get away from you or at least extend their arms a bit. This then gives you the opportunity to get out of his clinch or strike him.

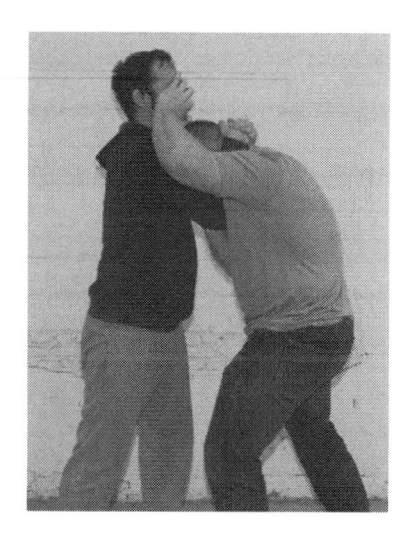

- As you go for his eyes, you can also claw his face open. The face has the largest concentration of sensory nerves in your whole body and ripping it open is painful. It can send an instinctive message to his brain that he needs to get away from you and therefore released his grip.
- Combine the previous techniques with violently twisting and wrenching his head all over the place. Used short jerking motions and direction changes to put extreme stress on his cervical spine and neck muscles. It is hard for him to use this clinch against you if he has to struggle not only to stay in balance, but also to suffer the pain of the tension you place on his neck.

Use any combination of the above or just one if that works best for you. As soon as you create enough space, hit him hard with the punches of your choice to stop him from getting you back in a clinch.

As a final caveat: *don't assume any of this is easy.* Fighting in the street is furious and chaotic. Expect him to not easily give up that clinch and be ready to keep on fighting until you can free yourself.

Necktie and elbow control

This is another common position you can find yourself in during a fight, in particular after a failed attempt at a double necktie. Here's how it goes:

- Face your partner and with your lead arm, grab the back of his neck like you did in the previous technique. He does the same to you.
- With your back arm, hook your hand into the bent of his lead arm elbow. He does the same to you.

This clinch lets you manipulate opponents by twisting, pulling, lifting, turning them and so on. It is hard to strike from that position with traditional techniques, because the neck control makes it difficult to get away. The elbow control makes it hard for you to generate power in your lead hand. You can punch with your rear arm and that is what most people do. Unfortunately, most of these attacks are not effective due to a lack of power. I usually advise against them.

Pointers:

- When you engage in this clinch, bend your elbows down. This engages the strong back muscles and gives you more control over him.
- There are a variety of throws and takedowns that don't take much training that you can do from this clinch, so expect your attacker to go for one. Avoid this by stabilizing your stance right away by bending your knees a bit.
- One option to break this clinch is this: explosively shove your attacker back with your lead arm. Before he can recover, retract your lead arm and place it in front of his neck or chest. Then let go of his elbow and start throwing uppercuts, overhands or even hooks to his body and head. As you hit him, use your lead arm as a shield to keep him from getting you back in a clinch. As soon as he lets go, switch to your regular boxing techniques.

This technique requires speed of execution and constantly adjusting your lead arm to keep him from grabbing you again. You can practice this technique on the heavy bag: push it back with your lead arm and hit it hard with the other.

Bear hug

This is often a panic move. Your attacker rushes in blindly, grabs you around the torso and then locks his hands behind your back. The real danger is that he can now easily pick you up and slam you to the ground. Or you might lose balance while trashing around and end up there anyway. As you know by now, not a good place for a boxer to be.

Here's another discovery drill for you:

- Grab your training partner around the waist, lock your hands together or grab your wrist and squeeze your arms tight.
- Then drive from your legs to twist, turn, and lift your partner. Notice how it doesn't take all that much to break his balance.
- Next, have him do the same to you soon know what it feels like.
- As you play around with this, notice how it is extremely difficult to develop any real power when some guy is holding on to you like this.

There are two types of bear hugs: arms locked in or arms free.

Arms in

This is your worst-case scenario. He controls your body and it takes time and effort to stop him from tossing you around. There is a high likelihood that you end up on the floor, slammed into a wall, or he holds you while one of his friends punches you until you're out. Because you don't have your arms free, you are virtually defenceless until you break free.

My favorite technique is to wriggle around to create some space, but as fast as you can, twist one of your hands in position and then grab his groin. Do so with vicious intent and with full power. Twist and rip with all your strength. Don't let go until he does but use any hesitation or openings on his part to free your arms.

There's no guarantee that this will work, but it is one of the few options available. Depending on his height and grip, you could try to headbutt him in the face, but the angle of your body might make that impossible. If it is an option, smash your forehead into his face but make sure not to hit him in his forehead. You might knock yourself out, so instead aim for the nose. That tends to disorient attackers, which you again exploit to attack his groin.

You could also bite his face, neck or whichever body part you can reach. Given the amount of bloodborne diseases that exist, I would save this as a last-ditch option.

Or you could mix all these techniques together, alternating from one to the other until you get free. Your goal is to stop him from lifting your feet off the ground and to break his grip right away. While you attack him, struggle and squirm violently and put up as much of a fight as you can. The combination of him in increasingly more pain and your entire body trying to create space is hopefully enough to get you out. When that happens, go back to your punching techniques to stop him from attacking you again.

Arms free

As before, immediately go for his head and eyes. Jam your fingers into his eyes, claw his face open, and wrench his head around to put strain on his cervical spine. Expect to hit the ground, because if you do this violent enough, it might make him trip and fall. Most people instinctively latch on to the person they're holding so they don't fall alone. If that happens, immediately get back up to avoid the fight on the ground.

Depending on how tall he is and how high he holds you up, you can also use downward strikes like vertical elbows, and hammer strikes. There is no guarantee this will work, but it is one of the few options available to you.

Conclusion

There are more clinches than the one listed above, just as there are other ways to defend against them. I don't claim that the techniques I explained above are the best ones to handle those clinches. But they are relatively easy to learn because they lack complexity. Unlike many other counter-clinching techniques, they also focus on breaking free instead of prolonging the clinch. This allows you to resume using your strongest weapons as quickly as possible: punching techniques. You are, after all, a boxer and not a wrestler.

To conclude this chapter, here are some overall pointers and advice:

- Clinching with the mindset of throwing your opponent to the ground demands specific body mechanics and techniques. These are different from clinching in a boxing ring with the goal of not getting hit and waiting for the break. For example, in a boxing clinch, you often see fighters lean against each other when they get tired. In a grappling clinch, this is a rookie move. Your opponent can then easily trip, sweep or throw you because the only thing keeping you in balance is him. All he needs to do is use your forward lean to pull you into whatever technique he wants.

    In a grappling clinch, you have to not only hold on to your opponent, but also maintain balance at all costs. That means being able to resist, absorb and use all the pulling, pushing or twisting movements your opponent does against him. The muscular contractions and the coordination of your limbs are radically different from those in a boxing clinch. You might get tired more quickly when you start training this way, as your body figures out how to do these techniques. Don't worry if that happens. Just keep on practicing and you'll eventually get better.

- Go train with a wrestler. Wrestling is one of the hardest sports on earth and its practitioners are not to be underestimated in a fight. Just like you haven't been punched until you receive a face full of knuckles form a boxer, you haven't grappled until a wrestler got his hands on you and mauled you to the floor. There is truly not alternative to hands-on training with them and I urge you to spend some time doing just that. Your goal isn't to become a wrestler, but you do want to get more comfortable in the clinch with people who try to take you down *and* know what they're doing. If you don't have a wrestling gym nearby, find a judo or jiu-jitsu class. The experience is slightly different from wrestling, but it teaches you similar things.

  A word of caution: be prepared to eat some humble pie. You can probably dominate a rookie fresh off the street when he spars in the ring for the first time in his life. Wrestlers can do the same to you in their arena. This doesn't mean you can't fight, only that you need to learn a different aspect of fighting, one that is new to you. So don't get upset when they toss you around at first. Remember that you aren't there to beat them at wrestling. You only need enough knowledge and experience so you're not lost in a grappling clinch.

- Boxing gloves make grabbing and holding your opponent difficult. Without gloves, you can latch onto arms, legs, skin, hair and clothes no problem because you can now use your fingers effectively. This changes the dynamics of how you fight in the clinch. Practice different types of grips and experiment with small tweaks until you find what works best for you.

- We all have a different body type. I'm a heavyweight, almost six feet tall and have large hands. My grip is different from a lightweight with small hands and stubby fingers. In general, the larger your hand and fingers, the more easily you can grab a larger object. For instance, I can grab the wrist of this imaginary lightweight fighter and fully encircle it, my fingertips touching. He can't close his grip like that around my wrist, which means I can strip or escape it more easily.

Do an honest assessment of your own hands and determine which kind of grips and techniques are most effective for you.

I cannot stress this point enough:

Practice clinching for the street, *a lot.*

It is by far the aspect of self-defense that is most neglected by boxers and where they all too often lose the fight. You don't have to become a wrestler, but you do have to know how to fight one. That means going on his turf, where you're not as strong, and learning how to deal with it.

Chapter Six: Goals and Tactics

After all the technical aspects we covered in the previous chapters, it's time to focus on how to apply techniques and to what end. What is your goal when you use boxing in a self-defense situation?

My advice on that is relatively straightforward:

Get away from danger.

Your goal is *not* to "beat" the other guy.

Your goal is *not* to "win."

Your goal is *not* venting your frustration.

Your goal is *not* making him pay for insulting you.

Your goal **is** *to get away from danger.*

Remember that you can only use self-defense as a legal justification of your violent actions if there is no other alternative. Nor can you keep on striking an attacker after he no longer poses a threat to you. This is a fundamental shift in mindset when compared to fighting in the ring. There, you go up against a trained opponent who prepared for months to fight you. He is ready, willing and able to fight and so are you. This is mutually agreed upon combat in a sporting context. There are rules and regulations, and you both want to be there. The goal is to beat the other man.

Self-defense encounters are not like that, at all.

They are completely different and so your goal also needs to change:

End it as quickly as possible so you can get away from the danger your aggressor poses to you.

You fight to get away from him; you don't want to prolong the fight. You don't want to score points. You also don't want to outbox him.

There are different ways to do this and not all of them mean running away because that isn't always possible. On the other hand, not every situation escalates to the point where you have to drill him with a fifty-punch combination for it to end.

There is a lot of middle ground between both extremes:

- If you can, just walk away. De-escalate the situation verbally and get out of there.
- If that doesn't work, use the least amount of force necessary that allows you to get away safely. Which technique that is depends on the specific situation, but if you can do it in one punch instead of two that would be best.
- If for whatever reason your physical action doesn't achieve the desired result, have follow-up techniques ready for immediate use. This is one of the strengths of boxing; you're trained to think several steps ahead. Use that mindset to have a punch ready for whatever happens after you throw the previous one.

Regardless of how many techniques you use, which ones you use or how hard you hit, your goal is always to end it as quickly as possible and get away. This is the definition of self-defense in most Western societies and if you want to stay out of jail, burn this into your memory.

My experience working with combat athletes such as boxers, mixed martial arts fighters and Muay Thai practitioners is that this is one of the hardest things for them to learn. They are used to the context of duelling in a ring or cage. That context means you willingly engage your opponent and always look for ways to beat him. You engage with the opponent over and over until you get the job done and are declared the winner. In the street, this is the wrong mindset. For instance, when you're in a confrontation and the other guy is about to throw the first punch, there is nothing wrong with dodging it and using that momentum to start running.

By the time he recovers from his missed punch, you're already sprinting away at top speed. Keep it up for a bit and you are out of danger.

In the ring, this isn't a viable tactic, so boxers never train for this kind of thing and often don't even consider it a possibility on the street. In self-defense *this is considered a win*; you're unharmed, you got away from him, and he can't get you. You survived and you're safe.

This is an example of how mindset is the hardest thing to change when switching from the ring to the street. I cannot stress enough how important this aspect is. In the beginning of this book, I mentioned it is hard to be both a good boxer in the ring and using boxing for self-defense at the same time. I have pointed out what crosses over in the previous chapters, but the differences between both environments are equally relevant.

Goals

There are several crucial goals you need to integrate into your combative mindset:

1) End it now. If possible, end the fight with just one punch. This sounds unrealistic if you're used to boxing matches that go the distance, I know. But if you go to the resources page, you can see several videos of street encounters in which just that happens: one punch is thrown, and the fight is over. It can most definitely work, but there are more aspects involved than just the punch itself. A lot has to do with timing, the surprise factor, shot placement, distance, non-telegraphic movement and so much more. All these variables are completely different in the street than in the boxing ring. As an aside, in the two upcoming volumes in this book series, I will look more closely at these factors.

In the meantime, practice your techniques with the mindset of creating an instant knock out. This has several implications. Instead of flicking out your jab to test the waters without doing real damage, use it to set up a power shot right after. Or use a stiff jab with a drop step to generate maximum power and knock the other guy down.

Don't get hung up on the example of the jab. Use whatever punch you like but aim to put an end to the fight with the first blow so it can't even get started. If that means knocking him out, that would be perfect. If instead, you hit him and his legs turn to rubber as he starts doing the chicken dance, that's good too. In both cases, you have enough time to get out of there.

2) Line everything up for your next shot. What makes boxers so dangerous is that they think in combinations. Any good boxer has a series of combinations he can throw at will and in a variety of circumstances. These can overwhelm an attacker because he can't keep up with the volume of techniques and defend against all of them.

Using combinations is perfectly valid and doesn't contradict the previous point. The trick is in how you think of them. You want to throw a punch with the intent of ending it right away, but if that doesn't happen, you're still in a position where you can immediately throw the next one. If your opponent is still standing after that first technique, you should be ready to launch another one the next instant. If that doesn't do the job either, the end of your second punch has to line up the third one, and so on, until it is over. You don't throw a combination for the hell of it, but only because it is necessary to end the confrontation and allow you to escape.

Simply put: if you need twenty punches to finish the fight and get away from your aggressor, there's something wrong with your striking. What you do is not effective and the longer it takes, the higher the odds of him getting a shot in. Standing in front of an attacker and banging it out is stupid in the street. Remember that there is no referee and if he knocks you out, there is nothing to stop him from stomping you to death.

Can you stop an attacker by just going crazy and unloading on him without thinking? Yes. But it is a high risk, high reward tactic. One that you just might be betting your life on.

Instead of fighting in those wild flurries, use the minimum amount necessary but make each one count and try to put him away with each shot.

Tactics

You have goals to work towards, so the next step is to figure out the tactics you need to achieve them. Here are some practical tips:

1) Orientation. A fundamental change from the boxing ring is that you can hit your opponent when he isn't facing you. I would even say that if you have an opponent facing you when you're about to strike him, you're not doing a great a job of defending yourself. The goal is not to exchange punches, but to land yours without him being able to touch you. A great way to achieve this is to have him oriented away from you while you're oriented on him.

Using a quick analogy: In a gun fight, you want the barrel of his weapon always oriented away from you while at the same time having the barrel of yours aimed directly at him.

Some boxers use this strategy to a certain degree in the ring by using good footwork and creating angles. This takes away the opponent's ability to hit them while they still land their own shots. One such modern example is Vasyl Lomachenko, the Ukrainian boxer and Olympic gold medallist who has taken over his weight class in the professional boxing world. He excels at using footwork to move out of range of his opponent by creating an angle with lateral and pivoting footwork. He repositions himself constantly so his opponents have a hard time keeping him in front of them. In the meantime, he keeps them in front of his "barrel", which allows him to strike almost with impunity.

Please refer to the resources page for a video of Lomachenko in action.

In self-defense encounters, try to always have your opponent oriented away from you as you hit him. You don't need to dance around the guy like Lomachenko, just get an angle on him and exploit it instantly to end the fight. Keep on reading for a few examples that illustrate this along with other factors.

2) Footwork. When time and space permits, use footwork to improve your orientation on your opponent. There are too many possibilities to list them all, so I won't. But let's take a look at a specific example to illustrate the concept:

You're facing a guy who is about to attack you. Quickly flash your jab to take away his vision for an instant and then step to your right with a single or double step. This places you at an angle towards him while he has to reorient to you. Don't give him the time; just throw your preferred technique from there with enough power to drop him.

This works well if you have good footwork, proper timing and you don't pause at the wrong time. As soon as you flash that jab, immediately start pivoting and stepping off to the side and strike the moment you're back in balance. If you wait or move too slow, your attacker has time to adapt and nail you with a good shot.

Notice how this footwork allows you to orient yourself on him at a superior angle and at the same time, lines up your shots.

3) Manipulation. Unlike in the ring, you can push, pull, shove and manipulate his body to change his orientation and leave him vulnerable to your attack. This works particularly well as an opening move if you know violence is unavoidable.

I like to use my rear arm to snag his lead elbow and push it towards my left. Use the power generated by a closing rotation in that shove, as if throwing a rear hand punch. This tends to rotate his entire upper body and exposes his side or even his back to you. It also leaves all his "barrels" pointing away from you for just an instant. Immediately after, turn into the other direction with an opening rotation and throw a strong left hook with your lead arm.

The body mechanics are virtually the same as when throwing a right cross lead hook combination. Don't retract your right arm before you start throwing the left hook, because that would give him time to recover. Instead, throw the lead hook *as* you retract your right arm.

Manipulating the body of your attacker is a way of creating openings to hit while giving you the time to exploit them. When done right (explosively and without hesitation), he can't avoid that lead hook. By the time he knows he's under attack, he no longer has the time to do something about it.

4) Manipulation and footwork combined. You can obviously use both concepts at the same time: manipulate his body while you use footwork to get a superior angle on him.

Here's one example:

A guy is in your face and points his lead hand at you. You know he is setting himself up to sucker punch you, so you decide to act. Simultaneously parry with your rear hand to move his arm off to your left and take a pivoting step to your right. As you complete the pivot, place your left hand on his shoulder or elbow. Don't push him away from you, just hold enough tension in your arm so he cannot simply pivot towards you right away. Most people instinctively do that, but your lead hand momentarily messes that up for him. That gives you the time to fire a hard right cross either to the side of his face or to his exposed ribs.

To make this technique work, you have to do everything in rapid succession. Depending on how much you twist him and how much of an angle you get with your footwork, simply pick the appropriate punch to strike him. Should he pivot fully and expose his back to you, then hold your left hand against his lead shoulder and fire an uppercut into his kidneys.

5) Safe exit. The fight is over when you're safe and sound back home. Until then, consider yourself in a high-risk situation. That means you also have to actively protect yourself right after you throw the last punch. This doesn't make sense in the boxing ring where the referee counts out your opponent and you get to celebrate your victory. In the street, bystanders get involved and attack you from behind or the guy's friends show up and jump you. If you're really unlucky, his mother might kick you in the face and have you eat asphalt (go to the resources page for that video…).

Exiting the scene safely is just as important as defending yourself from the initial attack. That is why I teach a standard exist strategy, the 360° scan. It works like this:

- After you throw the last punch, immediately take a step back, keeping your hands up.
- Take a quick look over one shoulder to spot potential danger.
- Then do the same thing looking over your other shoulder, taking an additional step back if possible.
- If you're safe, refocus on your attacker and assess the situation.
- Should you see somebody coming at you during your scan, act immediately.

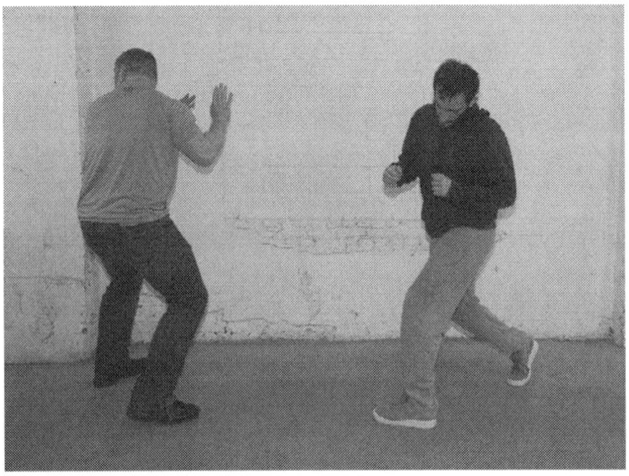

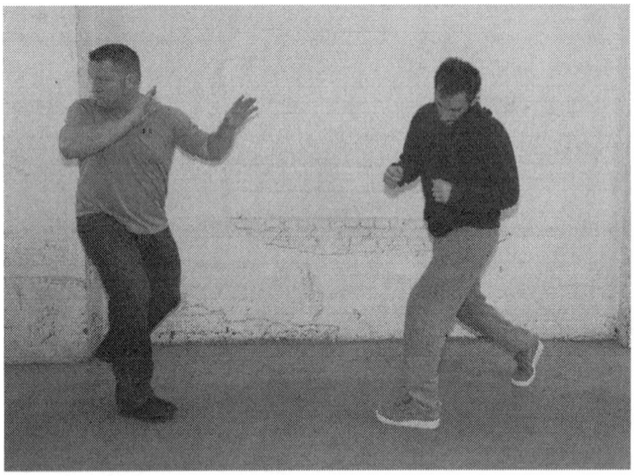

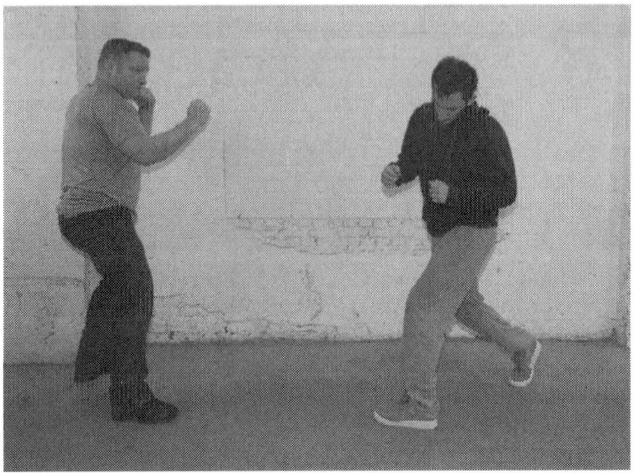

Nobody is immune to getting sucker-punched from behind or getting stabbed in the back. So when you train for self-defense, make the 360° scan an integral part of your techniques. It literally might save your life.

Self-defense tactics is a complex topic that requires more attention than what I provided in this chapter. The information presented is meant to get you started on your journey of taking your techniques from the ring to the street. This is by no means the final word on this topic. In the next two volumes of this book series, I will go deeper into this subject. For now, you have some solid basics to work with and can ingrain the tactical habits that keep you safe should you need to use your techniques.

Remember, the fight is only over when you're back home, safe and sound. Until then, stay alert and get away from danger as fast as possible. Doing anything else is not self-defense.

Please go to wimdemeere.com/boxing for what is mentioned in this chapter.

Chapter Seven: Common mistakes

Everybody makes mistakes; we're only human after all. That said, if a street thug wants to bash your head in until you die, it is probably best to make as few as possible. Throughout the previous chapters, I gave lots of information to make your boxing techniques work in a self-defense situation. I suggest you regularly reread them and systematically apply everything in your training sessions. With enough time and practice, you can master those techniques and have the skill to use them effectively should you ever need to.

Once again, nobody's perfect. That is why in this chapter I want to cover several common mistakes when it comes to boxing for self-defense. That doesn't mean you automatically will make these, only that I have noticed they consistently come up when people start their training along this path. So every now and then, check yourself to see if you are still doing okay in this regard.

Let's go over the list.

Ignoring the reality of street violence

Throughout this book, I repeatedly emphasized the differences between the ring and the street. But I'm afraid some of you will still dismiss this or think I'm exaggerating. The problem is that this might get you killed.

Fighting always happens in a context. You don't fight in a vacuum. That means there is a specific environment, there are rules of engagement (or there are none), there are multiple opponents or just one, and so on.

For example:

How many boxing champions are also kickboxing champions?

How many kickboxing champions are also boxing champions?

Look it up and you'll find there are very, very few. Isn't that weird? Because between boxing and kickboxing there are mostly similarities: you fight in a ring, there's a referee, you fight one-on-one, etc.

The biggest difference is that you can use your legs to attack. This matters because if you don't know how to handle kicking techniques, it is hard to defend against them.

There are also smaller differences. For instance, in boxing, slipping and weaving under punches works great. However, in kickboxing you don't see it all that much and fighters mostly stay in an upright posture. The reason is simple: if you use too much head movement to dodge punches, you get kicked in the face. Legs have a longer reach than arms, so while you try to get away from his punch, his leg can still reach you. This is not an issue in a boxing match because kicking isn't allowed. So, boxers can just ignore kicking techniques as a factor to consider in the ring.

In the same vein, kickboxers have to learn that in a boxing bout, it's bad to not use head movement. If they refuse to do so, even a beginning boxer will find it easy to land shot after shot.

Does this mean that boxing is better than kickboxing or the other way around?

No.

It means that in *specific environments, specific techniques and tools work best*.

The exact same thing applies between the contexts of the ring and the street.

If you take away anything from this book, understanding the differences between these two arenas is it. Switching between them requires specific adaptations in the way you fight. It is my sincere hope that I have convinced you as to why this is so important. I spelled this out here on purpose because I have seen too many young boxers ignore this reality and get hurt as a result. When it comes to your personal safety, you can't afford letting your ego do the talking. So please, take this into consideration when you train with the information shared in this book.

Hitting too hard

If you haven't used your boxing techniques in the street before, it's easy to have more adrenaline or be more emotional than during a professional bout or a tough sparring session. An easy mistake to make is overemphasizing power at the expense of equally important factors such as proper technique, position, timing and distance. You risk loading up your punches too much and overcommitting when you throw them. That in turn can lead to losing your balance, tripping and falling. As you know by now, you do not want to go to the ground in the street.

The second problem is that each time you swing for the fences and miss, it creates a window of opportunity for your attacker to land a shot. While you're busy retracting your punch and trying not to fall over, he can attack.

Do not overly focus on hitting as hard as you can. Power is only one of the many parts of an effective technique. Making sure you hit fast, precise and without telegraphing your intent is just as important.

Not expecting the fight to go dirty

What makes boxing so effective is that its training methods closely mimic the actual fighting conditions. Just as they do in the ring, boxers practice hitting with power, speed and precision while they shadowbox, hit the pads or work on the heavy bag. Then they spar and though that doesn't always mean hitting full power, it is rarely a walk in the park where nothing happens. When you add actual competition experience to this, boxers become highly efficient fighting machines with hair-trigger reactions.

The issue is that these reactions are calibrated for the ring and its ruleset. In the ring, you don't expect your opponent to head butt you in the face or throw an elbow instead of a hook, or claw at your eyes in the clinch. Though these techniques aren't necessarily superior to standard boxing punches, they can catch you off-guard if you don't prepare for them. Worst case scenario, you freeze as your brain figures out what to do next. If that happens, it creates a window of opportunity for the opponent to hurt you bad.

Don't give him that chance.

Expect the fight to have zero rules and every dirty trick in the book is on the table.

Not stopping in time

In general, when your attacker is no longer a threat or when you can flee, the law doesn't allow you to keep on punching him. If you do so anyway, you turn a self-defense situation into an assault. You suddenly become the perpetrator and transform your attacker into the victim. This applies in spades if you are more effective than him and deals out a good amount of punishment.

Is this fair? No. But laws are not about being "fair."

Reread Chapter One in which I explain the legal aspects of self-defense. Then it should be clear to you why still punching after it's no longer necessary can land you in prison. Stopping yourself from doing so can be difficult to pull off though, for two reasons:

- You're pumped up on adrenaline in a different way in the street than in the ring. It is extremely easy to get carried away in such a state.
- As a boxer, you are trained to think in combinations, to set up techniques so they land one after the other. In the ring, this makes perfect sense. In the street, you need to be more nuanced.

I suggest the following: have a specific goal in mind. Consider under which conditions you stop punching and then train for it. Watch the videos on the resources page and ask yourself what you would have done instead. Then figure out if it would be justified in the eyes of the law. Adjust your tactics and training accordingly.

My point is not that combinations are bad, on the contrary, they work extremely well if you use them right. The mistake I want to warn you against is using combinations and striking volume *without* regard for the potential consequences. You might "win" the fight but lose many years of your life while you rot away in a concrete cell behind metal bars.

Choose your punches wisely.

Ignoring weapons

A boxer's hands are his weapons, but not everybody you might face will be a boxer. So why would you expect them to stick to just throwing punches? Outside of the ring, weapons are used all the time. They are used as equalizers, to punish and obviously also to kill.

Ring boxing doesn't cover defending against weapons and to a degree isn't compatible with it. For instance, you can absorb an incoming bareknuckle hook punch with a shielding block. It might hurt your arm due to the lack of gloves, but it can work. If you didn't spot that the guy has a knife in his hand, then he just stabbed or slashed your arm. You might get lucky and not suffer too much damage, but your arm could also just go limp if the right tendons or nerves get severed. Regardless, it's obvious that repeatedly blocking that knife is not a winning strategy for you.

Dealing with weapons is beyond the scope of this book, so I'll leave you with two tips to avoid them:

- Watch his hands. If you can't see his hands, assume there's a weapon in them. Act accordingly.
- Don't assume he can only draw the weapon before the punches start flying. If you end up clinching after a few seconds of hitting each other, he can still pull a knife and you probably won't see it at that range.

This point illustrates why I always advise to either get away from the danger or end it as fast as possible: the longer you are in front of him, the higher the odds something goes wrong. If a weapon comes out, it can go spectacularly wrong.

Not leaving

After you win a match in the ring, it is time to celebrate. All those months of gruelling training paid off and you can bask in the glory of your victory. The fight is over and there is no need to focus on anything other than soaking up that glorious moment.

In the street, that can get you killed.

When you are attacked, the fight isn't over after the last punch is thrown. Due to the adrenaline and your emotions running high, you might decide to hang around and see what happens. Even worse, you could be so hyped up you feel the need to cuss the guy out and beat your chest to display your dominance. Not a smart move.

He might recover enough and attack you again. Maybe he gets lucky and lands a sucker punch, taking you out. Or he comes to the logical conclusion he can't beat you with punches, so he pulls a knife and charges in. If you're truly unlucky, his friends show up in numbers and beat the crap out of you.

All this and more can be avoided by one simple action: *leave*. When it comes to self-defense, the fight is only over if you make it back home in one piece and can close the door behind you. You go back to your loved ones and resume your life. This is always your goal in self-defense.

So if you do get attacked, end it as quickly as possible and then simply leave.

Conclusion

Authors write different kinds of books for different reasons. For me, this is a book of the heart. I have loved the Sweet Science since I was a little boy and a part of me still wishes I would have gone down its path professionally. Life took me into another direction, so this is my way of contributing to the body of knowledge on the noble art of boxing.

As explained before, this is Volume One of a three-part series. The next two volumes cover all the illegal blows, dirty tricks and much, much more. I understand if some readers are disappointed that they didn't read about that in the previous chapters. But doing so would have inflated the page count and required a number of pictures of epic proportions. It also would have meant increasing the price considerably to cover the printing costs. I prefer my books to be accessible to as many people as possible, so I opted for separate volumes with well-defined topics.

This book gives you the basics needed to transition from sports-fighting to self-defense. It can be a difficult road to navigate, which is why you need to train hard to ingrain all the concepts and technical details in the previous chapters. You know just how hard you need to train to be a good ring-fighter. Becoming proficient at defending yourself takes a time and effort as well. Use the same work ethic you find in boxing gym's all over the world and apply it to this new goal. Read a chapter and then try it out. Experiment on the heavy bag or with a partner holding mitts for you. Practice it with shadowboxing too.

Do the work.

At the same time, enjoy discovering just how effective boxing is when you make the adjustments needed to compensate for the difference between the canvas and the pavement arena. But most of all, make sure you stay safe. As a friend of mine likes to say:

Train hard, but hope you never need your training.

Good luck.

Author's note

Writing this book took so much longer than it should have. There were many reasons for this, mainly my health failing me. As I write this, my surgery was almost five years ago and It is been a long road to recovery with gruelling, daily rehab. This took up most of my writing time and energy, which is why the publication of this book had such a delay.

But I'm back to my old self now and have resumed regular writing. So you can expect lots more books to come. If you want to stay informed about new releases, go here and sign up for my notification list: http://www.wimdemeere.com/notification

No spam, just an email when a new book or video comes out and when I do a promotion/discount.

You can also join me on my Patreon page here:
https://www.patreon.com/wimdemeere

That's the membership site where I write a monthly members-only newsletter, post instructional videos, technical break-downs and much more.

I also have a small favour to ask:

If you like this book, there is something you can do to help me out: **spread the word.**

Write a review wherever you bought this book online, on your blog or in an internet forum. Tell your friends about it via email, Facebook, Twitter or any other way you might think of. Even if It is just a line or two, it would make all the difference in the world to me and be very much appreciated.

Also, feel free to get in touch with me and tell me which parts you liked best. Or the ones you didn't like at all. With your feedback I can improve my writing and make sure the following books are tailored more to what you, the reader, want to see. You can reach me here:

My site: http://www.wimdemeere.com

My blog, I'm pretty active there: http://www.wimsblog.com

Facebook: http://www.facebook.com/wimdemeerepage

Instagram: https://www.instagram.com/wimdemeere/

Twitter: http://www.twitter.com/wimdemeere

Thank you for your support!

About the Author

Wim Demeere began training at the age of 14, studying the grappling arts of judo and jujitsu for several years before turning to the kick/punch arts of traditional kung fu and full-contact fighting. Over the years he has studied a broad range of other fighting styles, including muay Thai, kali, pentjak silat and shootfighting. Since the late 1990s, he has been studying tai chi chuan and its martial applications and teaches those in his school, as well as a Mixed Martial Arts class.

Wim's competitive years saw him win four national titles and a bronze medal at the 1995 World Wushu Championships. In 2001, he became the national coach of the Belgian Wushu fighting team. A full-time personal trainer in his native country of Belgium, Wim instructs both business executives and athletes in nutrition, strength and endurance, and a variety of martial arts styles. He has managed a corporate wellness center and regularly gives lectures and workshops in the corporate world.

You can contact Wim through his website http://www.wimdemeere.com and at his blog http://www.wimsblog.com

Printed in Great Britain
by Amazon